American Education
in
International Development

The John Dewey Society Lectureship Series

The John Dewey Society Lecture is delivered annually under the sponsorship of the John Dewey Society at the annual meeting of the National Society of College Teachers of Education. Arrangements for the presentation and publication of the Lecture are under the direction of the John Dewey Society Commission on Publications.

THE JOHN DEWEY SOCIETY LECTURESHIP
SERIES —— NUMBER SIX

American Education in International Development

by

ROBERT FREEMAN BUTTS

William F. Russell Professor in the Foundations of Education
and Director of International Studies, Teachers College,
Columbia University

Foreword by   *62552*
ARTHUR G. WIRTH
Chairman, The John Dewey Society
Commission on Publications

Essay Index Reprint Series

BOOKS FOR LIBRARIES PRESS
FREEPORT, NEW YORK

Reprinted 1970 by arrangement with
Harper & Row, Publishers, Inc.

INTERNATIONAL STANDARD BOOK NUMBER:

0-8369-1786-3

LIBRARY OF CONGRESS CATALOG CARD NUMBER:

73-117763

PRINTED IN THE UNITED STATES OF AMERICA

Contents

Foreword

Arthur G. Wirth
Chairman, The John Dewey Society
Commission on Publications

While sensational episodes of the cold war and the probings of outer space have dominated the headlines, America's unspectacular but growing involvement in the educational development of the new nations ultimately may have a more enduring significance for human welfare. Our various efforts in international education have been part of our expanding responsibility in world affairs since World War II. We have gone through a necessary exploratory period in which we have gained experience and developed ideas and programs. We confront now the reality of long-range commitments. If we are to create a viable design for further work, the time is right for careful reflection and for marshaling our most fruitful hypotheses for action. Professor R. Freeman Butts, director of International Studies at Teachers College, Columbia University, is one of the best qualified Americans to help us achieve perspective and a clearer sense of direction. His scholarship in the social, historical, and philosophical foundations of education enables him to see technical details as related to matters of more intrinsic significance.

In *American Education in International Development*, Professor Butts traces the changing conceptions of our role in international education in the brief postwar period. Additional insights emerge that transcend the particular concern with education in less-developed countries. We discover once again that by being forced to understand events in societies other than our own, we learn important truths about ourselves that might have been missed if we had never left home.

In his study of the rapidly developing nations of the world, Professor Butts emphasizes that the change from a rural to a modern industrial society is essentially an educational problem. In earlier stages of our technical assistance programs, the educational dimension was viewed as peripheral to economic development or political-military concerns. Further experience is leading to the realization that social transition in the new nations has a contextual quality that will not lend itself to piecemeal treatment. Education, far from being ancillary, is a factor of intrinsic importance for successful change in all other spheres—political, social, psychological, as well as economic. This has led Professor Butts to describe education as the most regenerative profession, since all the others depend on it in a fundamental way.

As the details of the study unfold, one sees clearly the pivotal role that education must play in the emerging societies. But the same scientific-technological factors making for the social transformations in these countries are also sources of continuing radical change in all modern societies. The fact is that human life all over the planet is being transformed by a revolution in knowledge and its multiple consequences. In this condition, the people of the earth are dependent on education now as never before in history.

This situation mandates a kind of education that will produce people who are capable of continuing to learn throughout their lives. More knowledge about the educative process becomes then a matter of high priority. This accounts for Professor Butts' contention that a program of basic research about teaching and learning is as important for educational progress as the need for research in physical sciences is for technological advance. Our knowledge of the process of education must go forward as part of a broad research effort in which teacher education, the behavioral sciences, and the academic disciplines will be close and continuing partners. He argues persuasively that such research must be interdisciplinary and international.

Until such time, however, as we make the decision to finance such programs, we shall have to be learning as much as we can from a critical appraisal of our current efforts. One of the most important pilot projects in international education is the Teachers for East Africa program directed by Professor Butts. In the present study, Professor Butts gives a forthright analysis of the program in terms of the problems encountered and lessons being learned. It is a fascinating account of the complex of events in a venture where three educational traditions—African, British, and American have been juxtaposed in a common enterprise. The recurrent issues of our own national debate about the education of teachers inevitably become involved. They show up in the differing assumptions for preparing teachers in the Peace Corps projects as compared with the Teachers for East Africa program. Having been involved as a director of both types of programs the candor which Professor Butts employs in delineating differences should make a salutary contribution to responsible re-thinking now in progress. In the intercultural experiment at work in Africa, all parties involved have an opportunity to learn if they are willing to open their eyes and minds.

Professor Butts reminds us that development planning, which is necessarily concerned with weighty problems of organization, may acquire impersonal, bureaucratic qualities. Individual problems of the human beings in the schools may be overlooked. Rapid social change inevitably brings stress and strain for students and teachers alike in international projects. Young Africans are struggling to attain identity as they move from one way of life to another. By drawing on his intimate knowledge of work in the field Professor Butts recalls the special demands on teachers in these situations. In their daily interaction with students they are called on to play a sensitive and supportive role that can help make difficult human adjustments tolerable and healthy rather than destructive. Teachers are being called on to create what Lucian W. Pye terms "communities of modernizers" who can lead people to make their own way in a world of radical change.

One can scarcely avoid hoping that the interdisciplinary research advocated by Professor Butts might throw some light on the question of why the teaching profession, from whom so much is expected, continues to be rewarded in such meager fashion by societies everywhere.

The John Dewey Society for the Study of Education and Culture presents the annual John Dewey Lecture each February in Chicago in collaboration with the National Society for College Teachers of Education. The lectures represent one of several publication projects of the Society. In this particular series an opportunity is provided for leading thinkers from various intellectual disciplines to present their ideas on questions affecting the relations of education and culture. The John Dewey Society is particularly pleased to welcome Professor Butts's contribution to the Series as he has been a long-time member and officer of the Society.

Preface

Within the past decade American education has shouldered many burdens, but none more important, more delicate, or more urgent than its new international responsibilities. At a time when domestic critics have found no end of fault with American schools and colleges and with those who manage and teach in them, a growing host of "new" nations has turned more and more to the United States for educational ideas and assistance. I have been one of the many caught up in the centrifugal swirl which has sent to other lands hundreds of American "advisers" or "experts" or "technicians" under our foreign aid programs and which has now catapulted thousands of American teachers all over the world under governmental and private auspices.

Like many other Americans I was unprepared for the suddenness, the complexity, and the size of the tasks we are being called upon to face. Many of us were ill-prepared to respond as quickly, as surely, or as sensitively as we now wish we had been able to do. The sorry story of the unlovely and unloved overseas American has been alternately whispered and shouted for all the world to hear. I do not need to repeat it here, for its themes are familiar enough. Besides, I am now convinced that the record is far from being as dull or as lurid as it has sometimes been represented. Indeed, when the whole story of America's awakening to its international responsibilities is told, it may well be that the tedious and frustrating conferences by hundreds of educational advisers in the chambers of ministries of education around the world and the lackluster day-by-day teaching in the classrooms of the world by thousands of American teachers will take their places among the dramatic international endeavors that made a real difference in our time. Though some serious mistakes have been made with respect to our overseas personnel and programs, I have seen many Americans at work in Africa and Asia, and on the whole I am deeply impressed and greatly heartened by what I have seen.

Perhaps, after all, what began as an unpromising ugly American overseas can be transformed by the magic of improved selection and education into an international American educator or teacher who will surpass in promise, poise, and effectiveness our early fumbling attempts at "overseasmanship." If we take seriously our educational responsibilities I believe that the lowly American teacher or the highly placed educational adviser can do what the businessman, the government official, or the missionary could not and cannot do. Perhaps we shall find that the ugly American was an ugly duckling after all. If anyone can bring to real life the imagined success story of Hans Christian Andersen's fairy tale for children, it is a new overseas American teacher and educator.

It is this hope and this confidence that have led me deeply into the field of international education in recent years and have led to the writing of this book and to the lecture upon which it is based. Nevertheless, I approach the task with diffidence. I know that there are many Americans and many more colleagues and "expatriates" in other countries of the world who have been working in this field longer and more wisely than I. But I know too that the need is so vast and the demands are so insistent that the many more thousands being called upon to serve will find themselves still less prepared and less experienced than I have now become. Those of us who have had even brief international experience and training must make them available to others in order to improve the quality of what is yet to come.

Having responsibility for American education in general and for the education of teachers in particular, we must face up to the problem more directly, more effectively, and more rapidly than we have yet done. We must assess much more candidly than we have been doing what America's role should be in assisting those nations, both "old" and "new," that are seeking our help in moving themselves rapidly from traditional to modern forms of society, economy, polity, and education.

I have had the temerity to take on this subject in the belief that serious discussion of America's international educational policy will be set forward if some of us now deeply involved will expose our ideas and ourselves to widespread public scrutiny. My experience in international education seems typical of many in the American educational profession. If we lay bare something of our experience, our assumptions, and our intentions, perhaps we can stimulate useful discussion that will lead to improved endeavor both here and abroad.

In this book I shall try to face in several directions at once. The very nature of international education requires us to do just this. We must be concerned with the educational background of those Americans who are preparing themselves professionally, or should be preparing themselves, for long periods of overseas educational service as career teachers or administrators. We must train those who need preparation for short periods of non-career overseas service, such as the Peace Corps volunteers. We must reach the faculty members in American colleges and universities who select, teach, and train these would-be international educational workers and who teach those who will study world affairs in their home institutions. We must be concerned with the host-country officials, staffs, colleagues, and students with whom the overseas American educators and teachers will be associated in the schools, universities, or educational ministries of other countries. And we must address ourselves to the national and international planners or "developers" in our own government and in governments around the world who are making crucial policy decisions concerning the role of education in national development and the part that American education can play in that development.

To this end I offer my own personal experience as an illustration in a small way of the major stages that have so rapidly taken place in America's educational outreach to other nations. If we can understand ourselves better, perhaps our friends overseas will be able to understand us better; and between us the basis of our working relationships can be improved.

For nearly thirty years I have been engaged in studying, teaching, and writing in the field of the history and philosophy of education. As with most historians and philosophers my work for most of that time was based largely upon reading about the educational relations of one nation with another rather than upon active participation in them. And the emphasis for more than two-thirds of this time was almost exclusively upon Western Europe and the United States.

My first direct overseas experience came in 1937 when, as a young instructor, I was able with my wife's help to scrape up enough money to go to Europe for ten weeks in the summer. Together with another couple who were our closest friends we went by ship, tourist class. It was our version of the Grand Tour of Central and Eastern Europe between the wars. Despite the serious, semi-professional, and rewarding character of the trip, we were inquiring American tourists in Europe. In 1937 it did not occur to us to go elsewhere than to Europe—and indeed we probably did not have enough money to do otherwise. So in some twenty years of professional life I had ventured outside of my native land only once—to Europe for ten weeks. Prior to World War II, I believe this was fairly typical of America's educational stance with respect to the rest of the world. For some three hundred years we had been enormously affected by the transit of ideas and scholars to our shores from Europe and elsewhere, but American educators had done little more than visit occasionally or study sporadically a few other countries in return.

Then in the 1950s things began to change rapidly and drastically for America's international role in education—and for me personally. On a sabbatical leave in 1954 I took part in the new cultural exchange programs sponsored by the government when I went to Australia as a Fulbright research scholar in the philosophy of education. My family and I again traveled by ship, and this time we were away from the United States for nine months. The length of time abroad had increased markedly, and the distance from the United States had lengthened considerably. We touched the shores of Africa and Asia for a few hours at various ports of call, but basically our experience was still with the European culture—different as it was and is from that of the United States. My task was to study and learn as much as I could about education and culture in Australia—and inevitably to write about my experience.[1] A grant from the Columbia University Council on Research in the Social Sciences also contributed to enlargement of my views of teacher training in several countries on my way home from Australia.[2] I was now deeply involved in the first phase of America's new international role in education—the role of direct overseas study and actual exchange of academic persons.

Four years later I was off again for several months in the first half of 1959. This time the purpose and region of the world had once more changed markedly. A second phase for America and for me had opened. Now I was part of our government's new program of technical assistance to the non-Western world under the auspices of a university contract signed by Teachers College, Columbia University, with the International Cooperation Administration (ICA). I worked for four months in India with the Ministry of Education, helping to arrange for the role that Teachers College could play in the development of the National Institute of Education to serve all of India. On the way to India, the Ford Foundation had made it possible for me to glimpse some of the educational institutions of Japan, Hong Kong, Thailand, and Burma. Suddenly the leisure and delights of shipboard travel had disappeared; all the traveling was now by air. We circled the globe by propeller aircraft in a westerly direction, touching down only briefly in Europe on our way home. International education was now a stepped-up and more intensely serious business than cultural exchange had been.

Two years later, when I was made director of International Studies at Teachers College, I became committed to the expanded tasks of American education. Immediately I was involved in the third phase of America's international role in education, and another new region of the world had opened up for me. I suddenly found myself on the

[1] R. Freeman Butts, *Assumptions Underlying Australian Education* (Melbourne: Australian Council for Educational Research, 1955). The American edition was published by the Bureau of Publications, Teachers College, Columbia University, New York, 1955.

[2] R. Freeman Butts, "The Liberal Arts and Professional Education in the Preparation of Teachers: An International Perspective," *The Educational Record*, XXXVIII (July 1957), pp. 263–279.

way to East Africa. As if to match the new urgency, travel was now by jet airliner. In an exciting new project named Teachers for East Africa, Teachers College had been charged with the task of selecting and training Americans in relatively large numbers for direct educational service overseas. Under a new type of program of technical assistance sponsored by ICA, we launched the program just a month before the Peace Corps was established. Together, these two projects symbolized the opening of the third phase of international education for America. In succeeding months literally thousands of Americans were to go to many parts of the world not as educational advisers or consultants but as regular members of teaching staffs of the schools and universities of other nations.

This personally conducted tour is almost finished. During the academic year of 1961–1962 as beneficiary of a Carnegie Corporation Travel Fellowship, I was able to study teacher training in several countries of Africa and Southeast Asia. I revisited East Africa and went on to Central Africa, West Africa, Singapore, and Malaya. In addition, I returned to India, and then visited Afghanistan for the first time to inspect and learn all I could about the educational assistance programs Teachers College was conducting in those countries.

During my year's absence from Teachers College, some of my colleagues on short notice heroically mounted a program to train fifty Peace Corps volunteers for teaching in Sierra Leone. Upon my return I opened discussions with Peace Corps officials to see if we could agree upon a better, longer, and more professional program and if we could arrive at better ways of working together than had been possible in the first encounter. As a result of mutually satisfactory arrangements, Teachers College trained sixty volunteer teachers for Nigeria in the fall of 1962, one hundred eighty for Nigeria in the summer of 1963, and at the time of writing plans were being made to train other Peace Corps groups headed for teaching in the schools of Nigeria and Guinea.

In early December 1962, I was enabled to touch down in Latin America for a precious few days. The slow and late coming of Latin America to the awareness of many North American educators is regrettably another characteristic of our international attitudes in education. Fortunately, there are now signs that our educational relations with Latin America are being stepped up in quantity and quality along with increasing attention to our common political and economic problems. I am gratified that Teachers College was sought by the Agency for International Development (AID) mission to help with a program of basic educational development in the primary schools and teacher training colleges of Peru under the Alliance for Progress.

Finally, just a month before the John Dewey Society Lecture in Chicago in February 1963, I returned for a third time to East Africa where, at my suggestion, AID sponsored a unique international working conference to assess and plan for the continuing supply of expatriate teachers and to consider the plans being made for expanding the training of teachers within East Africa itself. At Entebbe in Uganda, the representatives of five governments and five institutions of higher education, both public and private, came together from three continents not merely to discuss problems and make reports, as all conferences do, but actually to improve understandings and actual administrative arrangements so that they could work together more effectively in the Teachers for East Africa project. The conference was beneficial in clearing the air of some of the misunderstandings, cross currents of national sensitivities, and personal interests that inevitably arise in a complicated international undertaking involving hundreds of people.

What I have been trying to do in this autobiographical review is to illustrate in personal and concrete terms what I believe have been the three main stages of America's educational involvement with other nations since World War II. The first stage, with roots far back in history, has been largely devoted to increasing our store of knowledge and understanding about other peoples and informing them about ourselves by means of systematic study in schools, colleges, and universities, and by means of cultural and educational interchanges sponsored by governmental and private agencies. The modern momentum for these programs of international study and exchange has greatly accelerated since World War I and especially since our commitment to UNESCO and the Fulbright and Smith-Mundt acts beginning soon after World War II. The recent upsurge in the search for international knowledge and understanding is little more than fifteen years old. We have learned a great deal in a short time; we must learn a great deal more in a still shorter time.

The second stage has consisted of providing technical assistance and advice to the governments and higher educational institutions of other countries through expert "technicians" in special fields of education as requested by the countries concerned—whether by means of bilateral agreements under ICA/AID or through such international organizations as UNESCO. This second stage is now only a little more than ten years old. For most of that time education has been pretty well subordinated to economic and military assistance in America's foreign aid programs. But there are signs that educational assistance is being viewed by AID as a more important element in America's foreign aid programs. Educators everywhere can welcome this move, for I am convinced that educational assistance is the heart of technical assistance in the development of nations.

Both of these stages in America's stance in international education are extremely important, and they have received a great deal of attention recently in public discussion and in print. A sizable body of literature is being built up around them. I shall have something to say about these first two stages of our international relations in education in the first two chapters of this book.

In the third chapter I shall turn to the third stage of America's effort in international education. It is scarcely three years old. The years 1960 and 1961 brought a new look to America's role in international development. Our government began to respond to urgent requests to supply large numbers of Americans who will become regular teachers in the schools, teacher training colleges, and universities of other countries. Overseas educational service has now been recognized as the greatest need of the newest nations in their efforts to develop the human resources upon which all other national development depends. I have given more attention in this book to the third stage than to the two earlier stages, because it has as yet had little serious and probing attention in the public press.

In the final chapter of the book I shall pose some questions that must be faced by the educational planners or "developers" of those countries that would receive as well as those that would give educational aid in the search for national and international development. I do this in no spirit of "having" or "giving" the answers, but solely to suggest a framework within which the cooperating nations of the world might jointly seek to work out mutually satisfactory answers. Chapter 4 represents the substance of the John Dewey Society Lecture as I delivered it in Chicago, but it was only one part of the broader theme I had in mind. At the suggestion of the Society and with the encouragement of the publisher, I have included the first three chapters in order to round out the subject. This enlargement has made the book considerably longer than earlier publications in the Lectureship.

Even so, I have not been able to touch any of the vast and important programs of education for international development being carried on by the private and voluntary agencies of many nations of the world, by UNESCO and other specialized agencies of the United Nations, or by other international or regional organizations in general support of the "United Nations Development Decade" as promulgated in 1961. There is much research to be done and there are several books to be written on these subjects.

My theme is simple. We Americans have developed the three stages or aspects of our international effort in education so rapidly, so recently, and so urgently that they have often been uncoordinated, indifferent, or even hostile to one another. We need them all. They can be far more effective if they support each other. They should not go galloping off in different directions. If they can be harnessed as a team of three abreast, they could become America's troika in international education, possibly the most potent vehicle for international development we could array. The success of America's role in aiding the development of modernizing nations may well depend upon the extent to which these three outward drives of American education can be mobilized into mutual support for the benefit of other nations as well as our own.

R. F. B.

August 1963

American Education
in
International Development

❧ 1 ❧

International Studies:
Priority for the Modern Mind

The most avid enthusiasts for the "American" quality of modern American education seldom realize how "international" it was in origin and continues to be to this day. The first schools and colleges on the North American continent were largely transplantations of European educational institutions. The history of education in the United States is studded with "foreign" influences—English colleges and grammar schools; French and Scottish academies; German kindergartens, normal schools, and universities; Dutch, Swiss, and Italian primary schools; Spanish mission schools; Scandinavian gymnastics; and Russian craft work. Not only did the first teachers and professors actually come from Europe, but when they became "American" in the eighteenth and nineteenth centuries, they continued to look back to Europe for educational ideas, innovations, and practices. In pedagogical method we have embraced many foreign "isms": English Lancastrianism, Swiss Pestalozzianism, and German Froebelianism and Herbartianism, to name only a few.

Even when we came to develop our own distinctively American educational institutions we often did it in response to "foreign" influences. The public school idea itself was designed in large part to solve the problem of achieving national unity in the face of large numbers of people who had come to America from different national

1

states, with different languages, cultural perceptions, social customs, and political habits. The secular public school was a response to the need to achieve religious freedom in the face of conflict and strife among a wide variety of religious outlooks brought from many parts of the world. The search for equality of educational opportunity and humanitarianism in American schools was made more intense by the range and variety of economic backgrounds that marked those who rushed to America to escape crushing poverty or in the hope that they could better themselves. Of course, we periodically threw off foreign influences, too, as we sought our own way in education. In the apostolic sweep of "foreign" ideas through American colleges, English Puritanism or Anglicanism might give way for a time to English Unitarianism or to French positivism only to be replaced in turn by German pietism, or Scottish realism, or German transcendentalism. Our intellectual and educational styles have never been content to be wholly indigenous—and could not have remained so even if they had been purely local in origin.

The point is that American education has been the beneficiary of foreign ideas, institutions, scholars, and teachers from its very beginnings. Their transit to these shores has a long and important history, but I cannot dwell on it here. For three hundred years, American education has benefited from the flow of people, ideas, and scholarship from the rest of the world. For most of that time we have received much more than we have given. Especially in the period when we were developing our own modern nationhood did we experiment with ideas and practices from abroad. We grafted the German university ideal of specialized research and graduate study with the general unspecialized goal of an English liberal arts college, putting both to work within the framework of a state university to help do the practical job of nation-building in a way in which neither Britain nor Germany had intended. We established European-type normal schools for training primary teachers and kept them isolated from the training of secondary school teachers in colleges and universities of arts and sciences as Europe had done; but then we produced university schools of education to bring their training together in a way that is not paralleled elsewhere in the world. In secondary education we followed the general pattern of the usual academic studies of English grammar schools, French lycées, or German gymnasiums, but then we also brought under the same school roof the vocational and trade studies that other countries usually relegate to "technical" schools. In the course of this process we produced the comprehensive public high school which still has no exact counterpart and which is being eyed, sometimes suspiciously and sometimes admiringly, by other parts of the world. We found value in the centralized school systems of French and German states and built our own state systems of education from the lowest to the highest levels, but we provided for decentralized administration in local districts and insisted upon a possibility for upward mobility not found elsewhere in the world.

I am not trying to imply that the rest of the educational world looks upon these institutions or these goals as unmixed blessings. Foreign educators find a good deal of fault with them—as do those American critics of our own system who find many more blessings in the schools and institutions of other lands. But we have built these educational institutions out of the intermixture of ideas and traditions from many sources outside the United States as well as within. We did this as a part of the modernizing process through which we arrived at our own distinctive nationhood. It is a story worth studying for its positive as well as its negative lessons for those nations now trying to speed up their own modernization.[1] Many "new" nations are attempting to move rapidly from a traditional agrarian type of society marked by widespread illiteracy, fixed or hereditary kinship and status groups, and localized loyalties in the direction of a modern style of society marked by urban life, widespread education, economic and technological development, and democratic political forms. Americans need to know more about what the other peoples of the world are now experiencing, and the other peoples of the world may find it

[1] See for example R. Freeman Butts, "Search for Freedom: the Story of American Education," *National Education Association Journal*, XXXXIX (March 1960), pp. 33–48.

of value to find out more about American education, as well as American science, technology, and development in general.

These efforts at improved international knowledge and understanding take two general forms for American education: programs of study about other peoples of the world undertaken by American students in their own institutions at home; and exchange programs in which Americans go overseas to study or teach in foreign institutions and in which others come to this country to study or teach in our institutions. This chapter deals briefly with these two aspects of international studies. This knowledge is an indispensable base for any desirable role that Americans can or should play in the international development of other countries—a role that increasing numbers of Americans are rapidly being called upon to play.

Since World War II the efforts of American schools, colleges, and universities to stimulate the study of other peoples, to learn more about them and their ways, and to promote firsthand travel and study overseas have expanded enormously. With the financial help of the great foundations and the National Defense Education Act (1958), special programs and centers established in many colleges and universities are only the most visible signs of a general awakening to the importance of international studies. A great deal has been written about these efforts, but I shall not try to summarize here the increasing volume of literature on the subject.[2]

ADVANCING KNOWLEDGE OF WORLD AFFAIRS

Many educational institutions are giving increased attention to teaching in the fields of international relations and comparative studies in politics, economics, and the other social sciences. There is new stress upon world history, the improved teaching of foreign languages, upon English as a second language, and upon comparative literature and linguistics. Of special interest to international development is the appearance of "area studies" which bring together knowl-

[2] Extensive and recent bibliographies on various phases of education for international knowledge and understanding are contained in the titles marked by asterisk in the Bibliography, pp. 126–128.

edge from several disciplines to focus upon understanding of the life and culture of a particular region of the world, particularly the too-little studied countries of Asia, Africa, and Latin America. History, political science, anthropology, sociology, economics, geography, and the appropriate languages have been especially prominent in area programs. Within professional education there has been a parallel up-swing of attention to comparative education and international education as such. I am heartily in favor of this general trend as a means of advancing knowledge and bringing it to bear upon American education in such way as to enlarge our perspective on the world and enable us to cope more readily and effectively with our new international responsibilities.

The reasons for this upsurge of interest in learning more about other peoples of the world are of course varied. Some stress the necessity for international understanding and international-mindedness as essential for world peace. Others put the emphasis upon knowledge that is needed by those who will be dealing with other countries in governmental, business, or educational matters and will therefore be useful in their training. Still others are concerned that America put her best foot forward and project a good image of our country and ourselves by going abroad as "ambassadors" of the American way of life. In any case, it is argued that we need to know more about the people with whom we must live in the world community.

In a report to the Board of Trustees of Teachers College in 1957 I put the case for increased study of world affairs this way:

American education should promote a wider and deeper understanding of world affairs among the American people. World affairs are every man's affairs. The urgency of the international situation is such that the widest possible understanding among the vast majority of people is a necessity that can no longer be overlooked. Americans need to comprehend the ways of life, the aspirations, the beliefs, and the values of other peoples of the world if they are to make sound judgments concerning the role of America in the world. Americans also need to acquire perspective concerning their own attitudes toward themselves, toward American life, and toward America's role in the world, whether they are individual tourists or professional representatives in other lands or whether they are stay-at-home participants in making America's foreign policy. In sum, Americans need to develop the attitudes and be concerned about the conditions of life that are required if different peoples are to live together at peace in the present world of national interdependence. Failure to acquire such understanding involves nothing less than the risk of war and annihilation.

Similar themes have been effectively stated in recent years by a number of the most highly placed members of the American intellectual and educational community.[3] I shall therefore not try to discuss the general role to be played by colleges and universities in this respect, but I am convinced that study of world affairs should begin in the schools below the college level, and, therefore, professional schools of education have a particular obligation to promote a more vital education in world affairs for all their students and staff members. Understanding of world affairs should be an integral and important part of the general education and professional preparation of every prospective teacher, no matter what his specialized field of professional study may be. Through well planned programs of institutional self-improvement in international affairs, the schools of education of the United States should contribute to improving international understanding among the American teaching profession at large and through them the American people. Most of the emphasis in reports on the subject and in our international programs of study has been laid upon colleges and universities. I think much more attention needs to be given to international affairs in the *schools*. One means to this end is through changes in teacher education.

Schools of education are being subjected to all kinds of criticism these days, some of it justified and some not, but one more criticism must be made which I think is justified. All students and staff members of schools of education need to know much more than they now do about the essential characteristics of the ways of life of other peoples as well as of our own society. All present and prospective

[3] For example, see *The College and University in International Affairs*, Carnegie Foundation for the Advancement of Teaching, reprinted from the 1959–1960 *Annual Report*; and *The University and World Affairs*, prepared by the Committee on the University and World Affairs (New York: The Ford Foundation, 1961).

teachers need a better understanding of the ideological, political, economic, and religious beliefs that both unite and divide the peoples of the world. They need to know more about the basic elements of foreign policy of our own government and of other governments. They need to know more about the agencies of international cooperation and control that now exist and might exist in the fields of economic, political, scientific, and cultural affairs. They need to develop a greater sense of individual responsibility and concern for understanding the critical issues of international relations. Special efforts should be made not only to work with college students preparing to be teachers but also with the present and newly appointed faculty members of schools or departments of education in order to raise the level of international understanding of the entire institution of teacher education.

As present graduate students of education take their places as teachers and staff members in school systems, in teachers colleges, and in other types of institutions, they should be better equipped to deal more fruitfully with their students, their colleagues, and the public on international affairs, no matter what they may teach or what their jobs may be. We should also be giving better preparation in international affairs to those teachers whose subject matters are intimately related with international understanding; namely, teachers of history and social studies, world literature and foreign languages, and college instructors in comparative education, international education, and history of education.

Direct experience along with systematic study could greatly enhance such a program. Students from other lands who are in residence in American schools of education are often experienced teachers in their own countries. They could therefore be particularly helpful if they were enabled to visit, hold discussions, or even teach for short periods of time in nearby American schools and colleges, thus bringing the life and cultures of other lands dramatically alive for American students and teachers. Conversely, the many travel plans designed to attract American teachers overseas during the summer months should give more attention to serious international study.

Fortunately, more and more educators are taking steps along these lines. For example, the New York State Department of Education in Albany has taken leadership in this respect by appointing a consultant in foreign area studies and initiating tuition-grant programs to enable New York state teachers to attend summer institutes and academic year courses in foreign area studies and foreign languages. It would be desirable if these programs could be extended to study overseas as well as in this country. Especially useful would be the establishment of overseas curriculum materials centers where American teachers and administrators could go to study and to prepare materials for American schools with the aid of national scholars and teachers of the country concerned.

Another hopeful sign is the establishment of a new organization called *Education and World Affairs* with offices in New York City. It grew out of the work of the Morrill Committee on the University and World Affairs and is subsidized by the Ford Foundation and Carnegie Corporation as well as by other voluntary sources. Its charter purposes are "to mobilize the resources of the educational community in the fullest possible development of American competence in world affairs; to encourage the improvement and expansion of the existing network of international exchange in students, research, and ideas; and to promote the highest degree of international cooperation in education and the advancement of education in other nations." I hope that the education of teachers will be given high priority in the new organization's work.

The New York state consultant in foreign area studies reports that less than 2 per cent of the six years of social studies programs in New York state secondary schools is devoted to study of those regions in which two-thirds of the people of the world live. This is a measure of the distance we must travel in internationalizing the school curriculum. We cannot wait to begin the process until students reach their college years. All Americans need to undertake such study; it should not be confined to those who go on to college. The training of teachers can play a strategic role.

Professional schools of education should do much more than they have ever done before in strengthening their faculties and their programs in the international field. To this end several key personnel either located within the school of education itself or especially assigned from other departments for their ability to work with prospective teachers should be available.

First, faculty members well trained as political scientists in international relations who would devote themselves to the problems of education and world affairs would be exceedingly important. They should develop courses and plan experiences that would enable teachers to acquire a better understanding of international and comparative politics, economics and international law, world power relationships, imperialism and colonialism, the foreign policies and military policies of America and of other national states, the ideological patterns of democracy, communism, fascism, and neutralism, the operation and possibilities of the United Nations and other international organizations, and the role that education can and should play in the international development of institutions and ideas appropriate to the modern world.

Second, schools of education should have available faculty members well trained in anthropology and social psychology who would devote themselves to studying the social and psychological bases of national and international behavior and communication. They would be concerned with helping teachers understand how different personality characteristics develop in different kinds of cultures; how nationalistic attitudes and feelings are generated and changed; how conscious and unconscious motivations act as determinants of national conduct; how group loyalties of religion, language, race, or ethnic background interfere with or promote nation-building; how attitudes of internationalism and appropriate behavior patterns are developed; and what role education can and should play in the formation of attitudes and behavior appropriate to the development of modern nationhood in an international community.

Third, it would be most desirable if schools of education had available faculty members competent in the international aspects of sociology and economics who could concentrate upon the tasks of education with respect to economic and national planning and development, modernization of society, human resources development, community development, and the improvement of health, industry, public administration, agriculture, and rural life. Whether the total effort to improve the conditions of life in a society be referred to as "community development," or "fundamental education," or simply "development," the role of formal education has too often been overlooked or neglected. "Education" should be seen as broader than but as including formal schooling as well as informal and adult education.

Fourth, two functions long considered to be essential tasks of particular faculty members in many schools of education should receive even greater emphasis as a result of the new partnership with the types of faculty members just described. Specialists in comparative education should continue to concentrate on the likenesses and differences in the role that education plays in various nations and societies. They should apply the comparative discipline to education by studying various countries and regions of the world with regard to their governments and political ideologies, their economic and class systems, their religious and social institutions, and the historical and contemporary issues that affect education. They should help to bring to bear upon education the comparative analyses and research going on in the several related social sciences and in the various "area studies" now so important in many universities as a means of understanding other peoples of the world.

As a complement to the comparative approach, specialists in intercultural educational affairs should concentrate upon the educational and cultural relations among national states and their peoples, the cultivation of cross cultural contacts and international mass communications, the improvement of educational exchange programs of national and international organizations (such as UNESCO), and the roles which education and educators can play in the building of a world community. It would be appropriate if such faculty members also acted as faculty advisers to students from other lands. They could appropriately take part in or offer orientation courses on America and American education for foreign students.

In so far as possible, the international emphasis should permeate the intellectual and academic life of the entire institution that educates the prospective teacher. Special attention should be given to encouraging faculty members from all departments of a professional school of education to undertake special training and overseas experience to prepare themselves for this task. The goal should be to have available in every department or unit of the college at least one faculty member whose special concern is to bring an international orientation to bear upon the work of his specialty as he deals with his students and his colleagues.

Schools of education should make special effort to expand their staffs to be able to handle the international dimensions of their task without handicapping the domestic program. Foundations could be especially helpful in aiding institutions to plan for such expansion. Teachers College has already appointed its first regular faculty member who was deliberately employed on the understanding that a regular part of his duties would be overseas service from time to time. Many of this type are needed. To aid regular professors in developing the necessary international competence and to aid in keeping the home instructional program at full strength while the regular professors are traveling overseas or engaging in educational assistance programs in other lands, appropriate visiting scholars from overseas should also be appointed whenever possible. In this way prospective teachers would have the advantage to be obtained from firsthand contact with the outlooks and insights of scholars from other parts of the world.

Many American colleges and universities have already greatly profited from the presence on campus of distinguished foreign scholars, but they have often been invited on an ad hoc basis for specific academic tasks and seldom are they particularly concerned or have special contact with the prospective American teacher. Every graduate school of education should plan systematically for continuing positions to be filled on a rotating basis by scholars from different regions of the world. Such visiting scholars could help prospective American teachers to understand and interpret the policies and aspirations of other countries and thus enable the American students also to gain perspective upon their own American life and culture in relation to other peoples of the world.

WORLDWIDE TRANSIT OF SCHOLARS

This brings me to the second major way that American education has attempted to build up its fund of international knowledge and understanding in recent years. We have sent Americans overseas for firsthand study, teaching, or research; and we have received students, teachers, and scholars from other lands into our own institutions. Again, I shall not try to add anything new to two recent statements on this subject which I strongly commend to all readers of this book.[4] I would simply like to point to a few places where I believe new emphasis is needed.

The outflow of Americans to foreign educational institutions has been of three main types of "scholars": college and high school students, college and university professors, and school teachers. Organized study programs abroad for American college students began on a small scale in the 1920s with a few going to Europe for their Junior-year-abroad; but far more American students eventually went for summer study or study-travel. In the 1950s the flow outward increased markedly. In 1954–1955 there were 9,000 United States students abroad; by 1960–1961 the number had more than doubled to nearly 20,000.[5] Most went, as Weidner puts it, to learn a foreign language, to make friends, or to acquire knowledge of another cul-

[4] See especially a volume of papers delivered at the American Assembly and edited by Robert Blum, *Cultural Affairs and Foreign Relations* (Englewood Cliffs, N.J.: Prentice-Hall, Inc., 1963); and a report to Congress by a commission headed by John W. Gardner, president of the Carnegie Corporation, U.S. Advisory Commission on International Educational and Cultural Affairs, *A Beacon of Hope—The Exchange-of-Persons Program* (Washington, D.C.: U.S. Government Printing Office, April 1963).

[5] Figures on exchange of persons are taken from *Open Doors 1963—Report on International Exchange* (New York: Institute of International Education, 1963).

ture.[6] By and large many of the organized programs help many students to achieve these goals, but Weidner found a "surprising lack of experimentation in the organized programs." He sums up as follows:

Most programs are young and only limited experience has been accumulated to date. Because of this or other factors, many programs have vague or diverse objectives, lack academic orientation, have poor standards, are inadequately tailored to the problems facing an individual student, and too often are not brought to the attention of students who could benefit from them. Though relatively few students should go abroad for specialized study, large numbers would find it advantageous to go abroad for purposes of general education or in connection with noncredit programs. The programs need to be integrated into the regular university departments and curricula, and into a student's educational objectives. Since there are many such objectives, study abroad choices need to be numerous so that any one student is likely to find a program that meets his distinctive requirements.[7]

Too few prospective teachers take part in the student abroad programs. The liberal arts colleges have been far more energetic in this cause than have the professional schools of education. In 1962 approximately 2 per cent were in the field of education. Possibly, the financial resources of these students' parents have a good deal to do with this fact; but it remains true that, if direct experience abroad is valuable for university students in general and if the American schools will profit from teachers who have had overseas experience, then more prospective teachers should have the opportunity of overseas study during their pre-service educational training. Teachers with such experience can have more "multiplier effect" than most other professionals. Foundations and government could well take note. It is probably likely that most American college students will continue to go to institutions in Western Europe and to other technologically advanced societies for their undergraduate study. This experience would make a good counterfoil to later teaching experience in an underdeveloped or non-European country (to which I shall turn in Chapter 3).

The other major outflow of Americans is made up of college and

[6] Edward W. Weidner, *The World Role of Universities* (New York: McGraw-Hill Book Co., 1962), p. 73.
[7] *Ibid*, p. 110.

university professors who go abroad to teach, study, or conduct research. This has been a practice for many decades among individual scholars, but it did not become a really large-scale operation until the government passed the Fulbright and Smith-Mundt laws of 1946 and 1948. In 1955–1956 there were 1,200 United States faculty members on academic assignment abroad; in 1962–1963 some 2,900 Americans were visiting the higher educational institutions of ninety countries. Most of these were in the fields of the humanities, social sciences, and physical sciences; all too few in the field of education (8.4 per cent). Special efforts should be made to encourage more professors of education to take greater part.

Finally, a small number of American school teachers have participated in exchange programs sponsored by the U.S. Office of Education. In fifteen years some 2,300 teachers have gone abroad to teach for a year in direct exchange programs, and another 1,200 have gone to teach for a year in the schools of other countries without specific exchanges coming to fill their places. It is clear that almost as many professors go abroad in one year as teachers have gone in fifteen years. This is an imbalance that is understandable but not necessarily desirable in view of the importance of international education in our lower schools as well as in our higher institutions. Fortunately, this imbalance will be somewhat remedied when the Teachers for East Africa and the Peace Corps teachers begin to return to American schools, but they still will not anywhere fill the need for large numbers of experienced American teachers who will have had the opportunity to teach as well as to learn from teaching in another cultural and educational setting.

The inflow into the United States from other countries through exchange programs sponsored by government and private agencies reveals much the same sort of unfavorable balance with respect to students of education, professors of education, and school teachers. The flood of foreign students coming to American colleges and universities has dramatically increased from an estimated 10,000 in 1930 to more than 64,000 in 1962–1963. At this rate of increase of about 10 per cent a year, we shall be receiving some 120,000 to 125,000 students a year by 1970. It is estimated[8] that the proportion of graduate students will increase greatly, so that by 1970 more than 85,000 of the total will be pursuing graduate studies. Again, a fairly small percentage (5 per cent) have come in the field of education at a time when other countries desperately need teachers. This is a complicated problem and not easy to solve, but it illustrates something of the worldwide character of the relatively low academic status accorded to professional education. One strategic way to improve affairs would be to encourage a larger number of graduate students in education to come to the United States. Many of the present leaders of emerging nations have been trained as teachers. This group is comprised of some of the most important and influential persons to come to this country for advanced training. The number of students from Africa and Asia going to Communist countries increased threefold—from 6,000 in 1960 to 18,000 in 1963. At a time when disenchantment with Communist-sponsored education is growing among African students—as evidenced in Bulgaria in February 1963—our doors should be more freely open than ever.

The number of faculty members and scholars coming to the United States has also increased from 600 in 1954–1955 until nearly 6,000 were here in 1962–1963 from ninety countries; quite naturally, most were interested in scientific and technological fields. Not enough university teachers of education or top educational officials come to do research or teach in American institutions (less than 2 per cent of the total). And since 1946 a total of only 2,500 teachers from other lands has come to teach in our schools for a year or so. This again is not an easy matter to solve, but we should try to make it easier for American children to have regular and continuing access to teachers from other lands. This would not only conform to our earlier tradition of welcoming the peoples of all the world to our shores, it could help to open up again the flow of national and cultural variety that has been reduced to a trickle since we closed the floodgates of

[8] John L. Thurston, "The Education Explosion: Foreign Student Enrollments in the U.S.," *Overseas, The Magazine of Educational Exchange,* II (March 1963), pp. 2–5.

immigration some years ago. Just as basic language skills and behavior patterns are learned most effectively in the early years, so could American children profit from the outlook, attitudes, and insights to be gained from teachers from other lands. In a later chapter I shall describe the effect of American teachers upon students in the developing nations. We have not been enough concerned to give our children firsthand contact with "expatriate" teachers.

Many institutions of professional education now provide regular degree programs and participant training programs for qualified students from abroad, but more should be done to provide international conferences or seminars for key educational officials who are visiting for short periods of time from other countries. This might include a series of international seminars for groups of educational planners or "developers" from various regions of the world. These might last from two to six or eight weeks at a time. For example, international seminars might be held for from ten to twelve persons who occupy important positions in the over-all national planning of education in various countries as well as for those concerned especially with elementary education, secondary education, higher education, adult education, or educational research. It would also be particularly important to organize seminars for junior staff members who are being prepared to take on more responsible positions or to take over from expatriate officers in ministries of education, teacher training institutions, and in the administration and supervision of education as their countries become independent.

Because of the wide variety of countries from which observers come and the nearly endless variety of American institutions, the experiences to be gained in the United States should be planned much more carefully than any one institution or any one government agency can now do it. I suggest that a consortium of professional schools of education supported by government or foundation funds might better prepare themselves for such visits and bring greater order and sense out of much of the present confused and hurried traveling that goes on in the name of educational exchange. The visitors might gain a great deal more out of their travels if each had an institutional home base in the United States and then visited other institutions according to plans agreed upon by those associated in the consortium. Upon their return to the institution of their home base the visitors would be more ready to inject a flow of firsthand experience and understanding into their conference work, seminar discussion, or individual study as they prepare to return home.

It would be especially important to enable selected foreign educational leaders to spend considerable time at one institution, free from the distractions and demands of their jobs, in intensive work on some aspect of American education or on some educational plans for their own countries.

The longer term training of educational visitors from overseas would be greatly enhanced if during their study here they could have access to the results of the ongoing investigations of theory and practice being undertaken in programs of international educational research which I shall mention in the next chapter of this book. The new knowledge could thus be put to the test of firsthand analysis and appraisal while the visitors are here and if found feasible put to work quickly and efficiently upon their return to their homelands. We would thus have a built-in process of interaction between research and training: research that grows out of the need for improvement of educational theory and practice; and training that rests upon tested knowledge.

This process could be institutionalized at appropriate universities by establishing a continuing seminar to deal with cross-cultural contacts through education. This cross-cultural seminar on education might continue throughout each year with a nucleus of regular staff members and research workers, but it could be open to short-term visitors and participants when appropriate. It could concentrate on a continuing study of the cultural borrowings or educational impacts of one culture upon another. It would try to bring to bear upon education appropriate findings in the social sciences with respect to the processes of social change and development. If it were open to long-term participants working under technical assistance auspices as well as the short-term visitors of the cultural exchange program, it could also capitalize more fully upon the experience and background of some of the regular foreign students already in residence in various graduate schools of education.

This process ought to help the foreign trainees or visitors to profit more fully from their study or their travel in America and help prepare them more usefully for work when they return to their own lands. While the rigorous process of analysis and research attempts to develop theory that goes beyond present practice, at the same time the study of the practical problems raised by the impact of one culture upon another could aid in the training of those who will be directly involved in the development of national and international policies in education.

Instruction and research relating to international education in graduate schools of education would be valuable not only for American teachers and administrators as they work at home or as they prepare to go overseas on exchange programs, but would be important to foreigners who come to America for the study of professional education and indispensable for improving the quality of our technical assistance efforts in the field of education. At least one valuable result of increased attention to international knowledge and understanding in American schools of education would be the improvement of training programs for those who plan to serve overseas. I shall refer to this later.

Our most competent observers consider that our exchange-of-persons program sponsored by the Department of State has been exceedingly successful. The report of the commission headed by John W. Gardner sums up as follows:

Looking back at the program's first 14 years as a world-wide activity of the Department of State, we believe that the Congress and the American people can feel pride and deep satisfaction that, although some improvements are yet to be made, the exchange program they conceived has proved so effective to their purposes. As it has developed in the course of these years, it has established itself as a basic ingredient of the foreign relations of the United States. There is no other international activity of our Government that enjoys so much spontaneous public approval, elicits such extensive citizen participation, and yields such impressive evidences of success. In a time when most international activities seem almost unbearably complex, hazardous and obscure in outcome, the success of educational exchange is a beacon of hope.[9]

This is indeed a heartening report, and it is significant that the commission not only recommends ways that our exchange programs can be improved but it also recognizes that they should be closely coordinated with our programs of educational assistance in the developing nations of the world. I am as pleased as the commission is with the evidence that our exchange programs increase mutual understanding, dispel misconceptions, promote favorable views of American life and achievements, and benefit the grantee in his personal or professional life. I wish, however, that the evidence were more conclusive with respect to the benefits to the grantee's home country.

Though I am convinced that study of world affairs and academic exchanges are extremely valuable means by which education can contribute to international knowledge and understanding, I am also convinced that they do not constitute a sufficient international role for American education in the development of modern nationhood. The underlying motive of much of our international study and exchange programs has been to improve ourselves and our understanding of the rest of the world. This is an admirable objective, much too long in coming, and still far too limited in scope.

Nevertheless, we have too often assumed that international study is really a one-way street: Either we go abroad to carry our message and our image to the world, or we welcome students from abroad so that they can learn how we do things and thus be more appreciative or at least knowledgeable about us, or we try to learn about others in order to be able to deal more effectively with them as we promote our interests in the world market or world forum.

In other words, in educational exchange the purpose has often simply been to derive benefit for the "sending" group or for the visitors rather than for the receivers or hosts. Cultural and educational exchanges too often seek primarily to serve ends defined by the senders or desired by them. And perhaps this is inevitable. It may be that we deceive ourselves when we try to say that we gain as much from having foreign students here as they gain from being here, or that other countries gain as much from the presence of American students in their institutions as the Americans learn from being there. I am prepared to believe that such rationalizations concerning the exchange of students may be a bit self-deceptive or disingenuous, but I believe that is all the more reason why we must try to manage the role of teachers, scholars, and "technicians" in our overseas assistance programs so that they contribute as much as possible to the receiving nation, recognizing at the same time that pure altruism is exceedingly difficult for any nation to achieve and that it may be difficult for other nations to believe that altruism on our part is a genuine motive at all.

This takes me to the second stage of American international education, the stage of technical assistance. The international knowledge being accumulated from our exchange programs and from research activities in the several academic disciplines is not only important for the general educational purposes of all students, it is indispensable for the improvement of our technical assistance and overseas teaching programs. It should be closely woven into selection and training programs for overseas service. Conversely, the imminent prospect of going overseas for hundreds of Americans in Peace Corps, AID, or other training programs gives peculiar zest and vitality to area studies or to American studies or to foreign language study or to the teaching of world history and world geography. There is still no motive for learning quite like the desire for knowledge that is immediately recognized by the learner to be valuable to him in a setting he eagerly wants to encounter. Would that all teaching and learning had like motivation. International studies can be put high on the list of priorities for the making of the modern mind and for pedagogical as well as for intellectual and political reasons.

❧ 2 ❧

Educational Development:
The Heart of Technical Assistance

The second stage of American participation in international education opened with the Marshall Plan and the subsequent technical assistance programs of ICA in the 1950s and AID in the 1960s. The motives were mixed. There is no doubt that technical assistance for economic development was seen as a means of assisting other nations to strengthen themselves and to build or rebuild institutions that would lead to a more viable economy and political independence. It was also clear that it was in the national interest of the United States that the nations so strengthened would be better able to withstand Communist pressure from inside or from outside their borders.

Education has only been gradually recognized, often grudgingly recognized, as an important element in technical assistance; indeed, education was often admitted to the university contract system only if it could be justified as contributing to economic development. The typical method of technical assistance to other countries has been to send experts, consultants, "technicians," usually college or university professors of a highly specialized kind, to teach and to give advice, to help modify present institutions, and to help build new institutions that could eventually take over and stand on their own feet without outside assistance.

The range of world developments that have created new challenges for American education cannot be described here in detail, but it was

21

clear that in the early 1950s there was no time to lose in reassessing our resources in order that America might keep up with and anticipate the rapid pace of world events and of world needs for education.

In the years immediately following World War II the persistent rivalry between East and West sharpened the dangers of another world war. When the immediate threat was greatest, the United States began strengthening its military position and its military alliances to head off the big and hot war. At those times of imminent danger, many people were not interested in the slower methods of education at all. Then we entered the period of the cold war and of ideological struggle. In this stage many people felt that education should be primarily a cold war weapon aimed directly at propaganda for combating Soviet communism.

Of course, both the military threat of war and the ideological struggle of ideas are still with us, but a new conviction has arisen in recent years. Whether the Soviet line "softens" or "hardens," whether the cold war waxes or wanes, whether the threat of the "hot war" is in the foreground or only in the background, it is now clear to more and more people that economic, political, cultural, and educational development will be paramount elements in any long-range resolution of international problems.

We now recognize that the direction in which the uncommitted peoples of the world will go may depend at least as much upon what America does in the fields of economic, technical, and educational assistance as it depends upon what it does in the military, political, and diplomatic fields. It may even be that the single most important element in world peace and security is education—not as a weapon of national propaganda but as a means of national and international improvement.

One of the most difficult problems is posed by the economic, cultural, and educational gaps between the highly industrialized nations and the underdeveloped regions of the world. As many nations take rapid steps to industrialize and modernize, they have looked to America and the West for aid, but they have also looked to Russia, China, and the Eastern bloc for technical help. Political, cultural, and educational ties undoubtedly follow technical assistance. And in a fundamental sense, the change from an agrarian to an industrialized society, from a traditional to a modern society is basically an educational process. Development, whether it be economic or political or cultural, is fundamentally an educational problem. "Technical" assistance is not merely a matter of shipping a superficial set of skills or a body of information from one country to another. When technical assistance really begins to have an effect, whole sets of ideas, beliefs, and customs are threatened by upsetting, not to say revolutionary, changes.

Many of the so-called underdeveloped countries of the world are more in need of rapid development of their human resources than of their physical resources. Above all, they need more well-trained political and educational leaders of broad vision. The scarcity of trained leadership and of trained educational personnel is one of the principal evidences of their "underdeveloped" character. They wish to remedy these deficiencies as rapidly and as effectively as possible. They are sometimes dissatisfied with the kind of education they inherited from their colonial past. They are therefore looking for assistance wherever they can most readily find it to aid them in establishing, improving, or expanding their educational systems. The United States in general and the American professional schools of education in particular should respond to this need much more generously and more effectively than they have yet done.

In some respects the most remarkable and revolutionary aspect of the postwar world has been the growth of a spirit of nationalism and independence among the former "colonial" peoples of the world. Americans generally have been slow to understand the profound meaning of this new nationalistic spirit and to realize that nationalism itself is fundamentally an educational problem. We have sometimes failed to realize that anti-colonial feelings are stronger among some peoples of the Mid-East, the East, and Africa than are their anti-communist feelings. And too often they look upon the United States itself as a colonial power—partly because of our historic alliances with colonial powers and partly because of the attitudes they have developed about American policies.

Whether the feelings of suspicion or of hostility on the part of some other peoples concerning the military, diplomatic, and foreign policies of the United States have been justified or not, the fact remains that such feelings exist in many strategic places in the world. The range of these anti-Western and anti-American feelings has been documented in many ways, but one great exception is often plainly evident: No matter what dissatisfaction has been expressed abroad about other aspects of American foreign policy, there has been considerable agreement that our programs of technical and educational assistance and our programs of cultural and educational exchange have been well regarded and could become still more important in the future.

In some respects the people of other countries have been quicker to realize the importance of American educational assistance than has our own government. Because of the need to convince Congress annually that it is desirable to spend money on foreign aid, government spokesmen traditionally stress its importance in supporting America's own security and interests. This is usually done by pointing to military and economic assistance to friendly nations. It has also been important to justify these aspects of foreign aid because they have been by far the most costly. Of the $50 billion spent on foreign aid since the end of the Marshall Plan, $45 billion has been spent on military assistance and another $3.5 billion on developmental loans. Only about 3 per cent ($1.5 billion) has been spent on technical assistance in the fields of education, health, and welfare. In 1962–1963 about $380 million was earmarked for technical assistance out of a preliminary budget proposal of $4.5 billion for total foreign aid.

In the frequent criticism of foreign aid it is seldom recognized that technical assistance plays such a small financial part and that on the whole it does not deserve to share in the public charges of failure leveled at other parts of the foreign aid program. Even the Clay Committee report of March 20, 1963 which has been hailed as justifying substantial cuts in the foreign aid program stressed the importance of the technical assistance programs in the following words:

The most serious obstacle to growth in many less developed countries is the inability of their people to effectively utilize the resources at their disposal. Technical assistance should be directed primarily at the removal of these obstacles and is the major means by which external aid can help develop leadership and technological skills—essential preconditions for development—where they do not now exist. In many ways as well, our technical assistance programs are the most direct evidence to the people of other countries of our intent to help them advance. These programs need to be of high quality.[1]

"TECHNICIANS" BECOME EDUCATORS

Fortunately, it is now clear that the American policy of assistance has gone far beyond the original stress upon purely military and economic aid. While the emphasis is still heavily economic and military, aid in developing education and human resources is at last being recognized as the most important kind of technical assistance that can be rendered to many nations, especially the lesser-developed nations. The enabling act reorganizing AID in 1961 expressly stated this policy as follows:

TITLE II—DEVELOPMENT GRANTS AND TECHNICAL COOPERATION

SEC. 211. GENERAL AUTHORITY.—(a) The President is authorized to furnish assistance on such terms and conditions as he may determine in order to promote the economic development of less developed friendly countries and areas with emphasis upon assisting the development of human resources through such means as programs of technical cooperation and development. In so doing, the President shall take into account (1) whether the activity gives reasonable promise of contributing to the development of educational or other institutions and programs directed toward social progress. . . .

[1] Report to the President of the United States from The Committee to Strengthen the Security of the Free World, *The Scope and Distribution of United States Military and Economic Assistance Programs*, (Washington, D.C.: U.S. Government Printing Office, March 20, 1963), p. 17.

(b) In countries and areas which are in the earlier stages of economic development, programs of development of education and human resources through such means as technical cooperation shall be emphasized, and the furnishing of capital facilities for purposes other than the development of education and human resources shall be given a lower priority until the requisite knowledge and skills have been developed.[2]

The importance of education in the development process is also clearly recognized in the policy statements of David E. Bell, administrator of AID:

How do we help [other nations to help themselves]? Let me discuss briefly the two major contributions one can make: money, that is, capital assistance, and skilled people, that is, technical assistance. . . .

Money is essential, as I have said; but we should never deceive ourselves into thinking that capital is the primary cause of development. . . .

The heart of the matter is not the availability of capital, but the availability of skills, of competence, of know-how with which to put capital to work . . . a school building without teachers would be of no value—it would be an example of idle or wasted capital. But with teachers, and an administrative staff—as part of an educational institution—the capital represented by a school building becomes alive and useful.

This is a lesson we are putting to work every day in the foreign aid program. This is why we place so much emphasis on helping underdeveloped countries acquire skills and competence. . . . to help establish institutions in the countries which can provide skilled, competent leadership for those countries, without outside help, as soon as possible. . . .

Let me mention finally a last group of institutions for development: those that have to do with education. These in my opinion are the most important of all, because education pervades every nook and cranny of the development process.[3]

Thus the basic position of the American government is that social progress and economic development in the emerging nations are not only what those countries themselves desire, but that they coincide with the interests of the United States, whose security is enhanced

[2] *Act for International Development of 1961*. Public Law 87–195, 87th Congress, S. 1983, September 4, 1961. (Washington, D.C.: U.S. Government Printing Office, 1961), p. 4.

[3] David E. Bell, a speech delivered at the Arkansas Economic Education Workshop on July 11, 1963, AID Information Staff Press Release, AID–63–148, Washington, D.C.

by the growth of independent, self-supporting nations whose social development and economic progress are based upon free institutions —foremost among which is education. The Policy Conference on Economic Growth and Investment in Education held in Washington in 1961 by the twenty Western nations of the new Organization for Economic Co-operation and Development (of which the United States is now a member) stressed this over and over again.[4]

In March 1963 sixty-six American universities held 118 AID contracts for technical assistance in thirty-nine countries; of these, more than fifty contracts were in the field of education, followed by agriculture, public administration, and business administration. Now that we have recognized officially that education is a most important tool for economic development and social progress, I hope that the government and the educational profession together can take the next steps to put into practice the belief that the educational development of a nation is important in its own right, not simply as a means to economic, social, or military development. Indeed, I hope that we shall soon realize that educational improvement itself is *the most fundamental aspect of any people's development* (including our own) and provides the foundation for all other economic, political, social, and cultural welfare. For peoples who need help in improving or modernizing themselves, the most rewarding assistance that can be given is that of educational assistance.

The interests of the host country and the sending country must coincide in some important respects if the relationship is to be of long-range benefit to either. Just as the sending country must respect the fundamental aspirations and cultural values of the host country, so must the receiving country reckon with the educational assumptions and respect the basic outlooks and goals of the sending country. If the two are to cooperate in *educational* development, there must be some important agreements as to the nature of desirable national and international goals, as well as genuine agreement con-

---

[4] Organization for Economic Co-operation and Development, *Policy Conference on Economic Growth and Investment in Education*, III, *The Challenge of Aid to Newly Developing Countries* (New York: OECD, 1962).

cerning the roles that senders and receivers alike should play in educational planning.

As the Communist countries rapidly increase their foreign aid programs the political motivations of the United States in providing technical assistance cannot be ignored, but the stress can and should be put upon the fundamentally constructive elements to be achieved for the nations to be served, as well as upon the national interest of the United States. These interests are well stated by Max Millikan and Donald L. M. Blackmer:

> It is in the interest of the United States to see emerging from the transition process nations with certain characteristics. First, they must be able to maintain their independence, especially of powers hostile or potentially hostile to the United States. Second, they must not resort to violence in their relations with other states. Third, they must maintain an effective and orderly government without recourse to totalitarian controls, a condition which in turn requires them to make steady progress toward meeting the aspirations of their people. Fourth, they must accept the principles of an open society whose members are encouraged to exchange ideas, goods, values, and experiences with the rest of the world; this implies as well that their governments must be willing to cooperate in the measures of international economic, political, and social control necessary to the functioning of an interdependent world community.[5]

The problem of technical and educational assistance is, if anything, even more complicated than political or military assistance. The problem is psychological and cultural. And it is a problem on both sides. Many people in the less-developed countries are torn by personal insecurities and doubts as they find themselves in the position of *needing* assistance. They are, understandably, particularly sensitive about accepting aid and about the conditions under which aid is given and accepted. A particularly insightful analysis of the psychological predicaments of aided peoples has been made by Lucian W. Pye of the Center for International Studies at M.I.T.:

> For the citizens of the former colonial countries, the lack of theories and doctrines of democratic development is especially serious and disturb-

[5] Max F. Millikan and Donald L. M. Blackmer (eds.), *The Emerging Nations, Their Growth and United States Policy* (Boston: Little, Brown and Company, 1961), pp. x–xi.

ing. Their problem is acutely personal, for they desperately need respectable and widely accepted explanations of their current backwardness and convincing reassurances that progress and dignity are possible for them.

During the time of their subjugation they could identify a single cause for all their misfortunes: colonialism. This ready explanation of their poverty and weakness contained the comforting suggestion that all evil was related to a foreign "they" and that the self was blameless. Thus it carried the implicit message of their salvation: once the exploiters had been eliminated, then all could spontaneously arise to realize the better life they had so long been forcibly denied. . . .

Events of the last decade have demonstrated the pathetic inadequacy of such theories. The European powers, instead of experiencing a setback on losing their colonies, have shown an almost indecent propensity to prosper. The new countries, on the other hand, instead of feeling a burden lifted from their economies, have found it almost impossible to obtain from within their own meager economies the wherewithal to support even the level of public services they were accustomed to during the colonial era. . . . Many of the leaders are acutely aware that the dreams and ambitions they have for their countries, which are often called unrealistic, are really nothing more than the commonplaces of life in other countries. When the goal is to do what others are already doing, the haunting fears of failure are related not to the disappointments of broken dreams but to disturbing doubts about the worth of the self.[6]

The other side of the psychological predicament surrounding technical and educational assistance is the accumulated set of outlooks and habits that Americans or Westerners bring to the international assistance encounter. This, too, is vividly described by Pye:

All the illogical reactions of race and class, of paternalism and pity, of pride and prejudice combine in various ways to blur the Westerners' image of transitional peoples. At the one extreme there are those in the West who idealize and romanticize the efforts of the new countries. At the other extreme are those who contemplate with horror the end of an old order and the "descent of barbarians upon the small corner of the civilized world."

We are fully aware that the complexity of Western feelings runs far deeper than the sentiments that can be articulated in the realm of politics. In some respects the fantasies of the West about the transitional peoples spring from some of the deepest anxieties of the human personality: the

---

[6] Lucian W. Pye, *Politics, Personality, and Nation Building* (New Haven: Yale University Press, 1962), pp. 8–9.

concepts of "control" and "frustrations" that lie behind the image of "explosive peoples" caught in a "revolution of rising expectations" seem to be readily related to the deep emotions that surround the mechanisms of control in the personality.

It is hoped that by frankly and openly recognizing the complexity of reactions and emotions on both sides of the process of cultural diffusion we can make possible more honest and more effective relationships. If relations between the industrial countries and the underdeveloped regions are to improve in the postcolonial epoch, and if there is to be a joint effort to apply knowledge to conquer misery, then those on both sides must learn to face reality honestly.[7]

Small wonder that international assistance programs have sometimes had heavy going. Too often these seldom-talked-about elements of the international encounter have been ignored or swept under the rug. Too often they have not been faced as candidly as they must be. In at least one respect, however, the problem has been faced with respect to the failures of Americans who have served overseas. It has been fairly easy to find examples of the ugly American who has been arrogant, aggressive, insensitive, and self-centered in his overseas performance.

There has been great criticism of specific American technical assistance programs on the grounds that people of poor training, low levels of competence, specialized skills, narrow intellectual interests, and self-centered personal qualities have been sent to other countries. Such criticisms have been carefully documented in recent years in such works as *The Overseas Americans*[8] and *The World Role of Universities*.[9] A careful reading of the latter book will also reveal major successes to go along with the resounding failures which have been eagerly publicized for one reason or another. Virtue is seldom rewarded on the front page.

On the other hand, I think we are now beginning to recognize

[7] *Ibid.*, pp. xvii–xviii.
[8] Harlan Cleveland, Gerard J. Mangone, and John Clarke Adams, *The Overseas Americans* (New York: McGraw-Hill Book Co., 1960).
[9] Edward W. Weidner, *The World Role of Universities* (New York: McGraw-Hill Book Co., 1962). See also Clarence E. Thurber, "The Problem of Training Americans for Service Abroad in U.S. Government Technical Assistance Programs" (Ph.D. thesis, Stanford University, 1961).

that the human and interpersonal relationships involved in technical assistance, and especially in educational assistance, are far more complicated and deep-running than has been widely realized to date.

It is a relationship we must not enter lightly. We shall need all the resources of scholarship and organization and insight we can marshal to improve our technical assistance programs and bring them to the level of accomplishment required by their importance to other nations and to ourselves.

The books just mentioned and a good many more have described American technical assistance programs and made useful suggestions about the ways to improve the selection and training of Americans for overseas work. They give a good deal of attention to the role of American universities in relation to the United States government, to the host countries, and to private foundations, and agencies. The major investigations upon which these books are based were made before the launching of America's large-scale enterprises for sending teachers overseas as embodied in the Teachers for East Africa project and the Peace Corps. They therefore reflect the first and second stages of American international education, but not the third. They stress the university professor overseas, not the elementary or secondary school teacher.

Weidner found that the results were disappointing when university professors simply taught classes in overseas institutions and did not train counterparts to run the new institutions that were being built. I can agree that institution-building is a prime function of technical assistance, but I believe that educational assistance may call for both teaching and advice or consultation more often than they are called for in any other kind of technical assistance. Much depends upon the stage of educational development of the country concerned. In Afghanistan the Teachers College team has combined several functions: advice and consultation in building an institute of education and a faculty of education as part of the University of Kabul; teaching English in the university faculties of Letters and of Science in order to prepare Afghans to take over teaching positions in the university; the preparation of materials and demonstration of them in teacher-training institutions and in in-service courses for teachers; and direct teaching of English in the secondary schools until Afghan teachers of English can be produced in sufficient quantities to run their own classrooms.

In India, on the other hand, the Teachers College team has concentrated upon cooperative consultation in the building of the National Institute of Education. "Building" in this sense has embodied direct cooperative work on joint committees in which Indians and Americans have learned to work together as full-fledged colleagues in formulating entire courses of study, syllabuses, and examinations for particular subjects, and preparing instructional materials of many kinds for use in formal and informal situations. In both cases promising young Afghans and Indians have been appointed by their governments to positions of responsibility in the respective institutes and have come to Teachers College as participants to develop further their competence in the fields of knowledge required by the positions of educational leadership to which they will return.

In general, the smaller the pool of trained manpower and the less extensive the educational structure of a nation, the more necessary and useful will be direct teaching by expatriates. Such teaching may be as necessary at the secondary school level as it is at the university level; in East Africa secondary school teachers are more immediately required than are university teachers. This situation is likely to characterize many traditional societies. At the other extreme, the greater the pool of trained manpower and the more extensive the educational structure (as in rapidly modernizing socieities), the more useful and desirable will be the high level advisers. In between, in the transitional societies, both teaching and technical advice may be necessary in order to help educate the needed manpower and at the same time to help build the institutions that will continue such training in the future.

These two functions must be coordinated, planned, and conducted jointly. At the heart of educational assistance is the direct teaching that will help to produce a larger corps of future teachers, as well as the building of teacher training institutions manned with a highly trained staff who can take over the job. Those who take part in technical assistance programs for teacher education may need to look both ways—to actual teaching of students and to the training of the trainers. Whatever may be the distinctive role of a university in the United States, the heart of the function of an American university in overseas assistance is the education and training of those who will in turn be educating and training others.

I agree with Weidner that universities in technical assistance programs should be as free as possible of specific government restrictions and day-by-day supervision by the ICA/AID missions. American universities must be free to deal with their counterpart institutions in host countries, even when these governments exert fairly close supervision over their universities. Living examples of university autonomy and responsible public action can be most valuable for both governments. Especially valuable is continuing inter-university affiliation across national boundaries.

For example, the Afro-Anglo-American Program in Teacher Education supported by the Carnegie Corporation of New York has enabled Teachers College, the Institute of Education of the University of London, and eight institutes or departments of education in university-level institutes of Africa to build valuable institutional connections. Existing outside government contractual arrangements, this relationship has given these institutions an opportunity to establish operating procedures, exchange staff members, and arrive at mutual understandings of great importance. Indeed, it led to the selection of Teachers College and other member institutions for important roles in the AID-sponsored Teachers for East Africa project and to Peace Corps training programs for Sierra Leone and Nigeria. In such ways as this the longer term values of inter-university associations can help to overcome gaps in government technical assistance projects. Durable or long-term government projects are not always as politically or financially feasible as are direct inter-institutional ones.

Especially important, too, is Weidner's recommendation that institutions from the United States and the host countries be brought into the planning for technical assistance programs at an earlier date than has been usual. Too often the early planning has been solely by government officials. I can speak with considerable feeling on this point. I credit much of the success of the Teachers for East Africa project to the fact that representatives of Teachers College, the ICA desk in Washington, and the ICA mission in East Africa traveled together throughout East Africa exploring the possibility of the project before a contract was signed. We were thus able to build a contract that was professionally and academically desirable to the universities involved, as well as politically and financially satisfactory to the governments involved. What we learned about contract-making in that experience has also had beneficial influence in achieving desirable flexibility in our older contracts for Afghanistan and India, as well as in the newer ones for Peru and the Peace Corps.

It is heartening to know that a high-level exploration of the long-term course of cooperation and mutual contributions as well as the range of problems that have arisen between American universities and AID has recently been undertaken. David E. Bell asked John W. Gardner to organize the Task Force on AID-University Relationships which consists of twenty-one members drawn from AID, the Executive Office of the President, the American university community, and Education and World Affairs. It began its work in July 1963.

Fundamental to all other improvement of technical assistance programs is the selection and training of people for more effective performance of overseas jobs. Valuable proposals for improving the training of American overseas personnel have grown out of several important studies. Harlan Cleveland, assistant secretary of state for International Organizations, and his former colleagues at Syracuse made a significant start in *The Overseas Americans* with their formulation of the five gauges by which to measure success in overseas operations: technical skill, belief in mission, cultural empathy, a sense of politics, and organizational ability. Contrary to some common impressions, they found ICA people had relatively high ratings in technical skill and cultural empathy. They were relatively low, however, in a sense for politics and organizational ability. The authors recognized that elementary and secondary education may have a bearing upon the attitudes necessary for overseas service, but they concentrated in their book, as most writers have done, almost exclusively upon higher education.

The Cleveland book does mention the importance of training for overseas service in *professional* schools:

The internationalization of the university cannot, of course, stop with the liberal arts college and the graduate area programs. Every professional school, and every graduate program in the social sciences, must in time reflect in its curriculum the recognition that some of its students will practice their profession abroad, by building into its technical field of study an awareness of world-wide developments in that field, an interest in the experience that members of its own profession are having abroad, and an emphasis on the breadth and adaptability that constitute the "plus" of transplanted technical skill. With overseas assignments in mind, it may have to plan to turn out more general practitioners than ever before.[10]

The need is for a broadened range of subject matter, a deeper interest in technical developments in the underdeveloped world, a lively awareness that every overseas program seems to involve the specialist in that "generalist" form of activity we have called the building of institutions. There is plenty of room for study and work experiences abroad, for internships in American overseas operations, for the development of opportunities to study and work *inside* the institutions (the hospitals, the schools, the factories, the agricultural experiment stations) of a foreign society.[11]

These are useful suggestions, but I doubt if Cleveland and his colleagues thought much about their specific application to professional schools of education. In fact, few who have written on the subject have paid much attention to teacher education. Yet I believe that professional education lies at the heart of the technical assistance problem.

The university graduate schools of education should take special leadership in improving the quality of advisers and consultants who venture forth in the field of educational assistance, now coming to be called "development education." Closer cooperation between the university schools of education, the university regional or area

[10] Cleveland et al., op. cit., p. 233.
[11] Ibid., p. 298.

institutes, and the university schools of international affairs or centers of international studies is a necessity in achieving this goal. I know that this is happening in several places. At Columbia University, relations between Teachers College and the School of International Affairs are especially cordial. Nearly all of the university regional institutes and programs now have faculty members from Teachers College closely associated with them, and dozens of faculty members of university graduate departments and institutes have taken part in the special training programs we have undertaken for the Teachers for East Africa project and the Peace Corps. In the new Institute for Education in Africa, recently established at Teachers College, the director of the Columbia University Program of Studies on Africa will be a regular staff member, will offer courses on Africa at Teachers College, and will collaborate in a new course on African education and politics with the specialist on African education at Teachers College.

If Americans and non-Americans are to work together cooperatively and with mutual benefit as "educational developers" or "educational strategists," they will need to know more about the educational systems and programs, as well as the political, economic, and cultural characteristics of their respective countries. They need to learn how to work in such international agencies as the United Nations and UNESCO. They need to know more about the best ways that different cultures learn from each other and how they can aid each other in educational improvement. They need to become experts in the art and practice of consultation. They need to learn the best ways to mobilize people to improve their social and economic conditions and to make use of the role that formal and informal education can play in community and national development.

In these ways graduate schools of education should take leadership in providing better preparation for those who are asked to aid in planning, designing, and operating educational programs where they are most needed in the world.

For Americans who are planning on long-term professional careers in overseas educational service, professional schools of education should provide well-rounded degree programs, not only in comparative education, international education, and educational development, but also in subject matter and professional fields particularly needed in the emerging nations. Furthermore, they should offer short-term intensive courses for faculty members, teachers, students, or officials who are about to go abroad on short notice or who are home on leave from foreign assignments. Special attention should be given to pre-service orientation seminars designed for new education advisers of AID or university contract personnel assigned to overseas educational service. It would be desirable, if possible, for non-governmental workers to be served as well, for each type needs to know about the work of the other. Furthermore, AID education advisers and educational technicians already in service might profitably spend a short time or even a year of study while on long service or sabbatical leave.

One further point having to do with professional competence in job success, and one often stressed by Weidner in his comprehensive study, has been widely overlooked in training programs of overseas personnel. Weidner points out that the overseas professors in technical assistance programs were generally competent in the mastery of subject matter in their special fields, but the fields were so narrowly defined that the professor was often not prepared for the wide range of jobs expected of him. He needed to be teacher, researcher, consultant, and administrator rolled into one. Few had any experience or training at home that prepared him for such versatility.

But, above all, Weidner found that

The greatest professional shortcoming of American professors abroad was their competence as educators; most had had little opportunity to reflect about higher education as a whole either at home or abroad before their assignment overseas. American professors seldom have had any formal training in American or comparative higher education. . . .
When research and teaching were the activities concerned, most of the professors overseas performed acceptably. There were notable shortcomings in administrative ability on the part of the chief adviser, and in consulting ability on the part of those expected to use that means. A consultant is of necessity "other-oriented"; few university professors excel in this trait. The typical Western state university political scientist sent to the Middle

East not only broadened his field, but changed from a teacher-researcher to a consultant-administrator.[12]

Higher education is more than a combination of specialized subject matter areas. To be an educator requires knowledge of educational processes as a whole and an appreciation of the role that universities play in society. The professor who has taken time to understand the entire system of American education, for example, is much better qualified for an overseas post than a person who remains merely a subject matter specialist. If an educator-professor understands the relation of his specialty to one system of higher education, he is in a better position to become acquainted with the main features of the host-country's system and to associate with it. He may even be able to suggest modifications in both systems as the result of his experiences. Breadth of knowledge as an educator may be more important than specialized knowledge of a subject.[13]

This then points to another role for professional schools of education; namely, to give attention to analysis and study of the processes of education as a whole, the role of education in American society as compared and contrasted with the role of education in the host country, and the problems that arise when people with one set of educational assumptions come face to face with people who have another set. Not only do all technical assistance professors need to apply themselves to the comparative study of culture, politics, and administration, as Cleveland recommends, they also need to be professor-educators, as Weidner recommends. This is not only true of those who will be dealing with educational assistance in a narrow, formal sense—as applied to educational institutions—but it is also true of those who deal with educational assistance in the broadest informal sense, making it almost coextensive with technical assistance itself. We have not yet fully recognized that technical assistance is fundamentally educational in character. Introducing mechanized farming or building a steel plant in an underdeveloped country is not simply a matter of training untutored people how to manage unfamiliar machines. When inherited beliefs and customs are confronted by rapid industrialization, the people involved need more than training in a

[12] Weidner, op. cit., p. 231.
[13] Ibid., p. 225.

few specialized skills; they need a much broader and more fundamental "education" in new ways of thinking and behaving if the processes of modernization, national development, and international cooperation are to be successful. All those involved in technical assistance must be educators; for the essence of technical assistance is educational assistance.

NARROWING THE RESEARCH GAP

Underlying all other means of improving our technical assistance programs is the need for continuing fundamental research in order to create a body of tested knowledge upon which to base the improvement of education so as to strengthen the economic, political, cultural, and national development of the peoples of the world. Such research should marshal the resources of scholarship in the social sciences and should probe deeply into the fundamental interrelationships of education and social change. It should synthesize what has already been learned about educational cooperation; it should utilize what is being learned by the social scientists about social change; and it should bring this knowledge to bear upon the problems of education and modern nationhood in the various parts of the world. The cooperation of scholars from different national and cultural backgrounds, especially those from countries that are themselves being studied, is as essential as the cooperation of scholars representing different academic disciplines.

For the most part, the results of the "educational" activities of our technical assistance programs, as broadly defined, have not been systematically studied or carefully evaluated; nor has enough been done to assess the specific activities more readily recognizable as "Educational"; namely, explicit aid to school systems, teacher training institutions, and universities. Fifteen years of extensive but disparate international educational activity is awaiting analysis, interpretation, evaluation, and rationalization. Meanwhile, and often unrelated to our action-oriented programs, universities have accelerated their scholarly studies and fundamental research in international affairs and social change. These programs have been marked by a rapid accumulation of empirical knowledge and by new formulations of theory in the several social sciences.

Much of this scholarly work is being produced by university schools of international affairs and by regular academic departments in such fields as political science, international relations, economics, anthropology, sociology, history, psychology, foreign languages, and literature. In addition, special study of particular regions of the world goes on in the newly created "area institutes" such as those at Harvard, Columbia, Princeton, Yale, Pennsylvania, Cornell, Michigan, Chicago, California, and Washington. Also, study of a wide range of related problems has been undertaken at special centers devoted to international studies at M.I.T., Harvard, Princeton, Stanford, and elsewhere.

I have been particularly impressed by the studies of the modernization process that have been coming from the Center for International Studies at M.I.T., where economists have been joined by political scientists, sociologists, anthropologists, and social psychologists to undertake fundamental studies of the processes of social change but with an eye cocked on important questions of national and international policy.[14]

The theories of the modernization process being developed in these studies and in other important works[15] are extremely interesting as they seek to formulate the stages of political and economic development through which societies pass as they move from traditional forms of organization and outlook through various stages of transition to modern forms of society and behavior. Even though the rigorous processes of inquiry characteristic of mathematical theory in the physical sciences may not be duplicated, the effort of the social scientists to clarify, categorize, classify, and predict is nonetheless exceedingly worthwhile. Especially valuable is the effort to bring together into

[14] See, for example, the titles in the Bibliography by Coelho, Hagen, Isaacs, Lerner, Millikan, Pye, Rivkin, Rostow, and Shils, pp. 126–128.

[15] See, for example, Gabriel A. Almond and James S. Coleman (eds.), The Politics of the Developing Areas (Princeton, N.J.: Princeton University Press, 1960); and The Brookings Institution, Development of the Emerging Countries; an Agenda for Research (Washington, D.C.: The Brookings Institution, 1962).

some coherent whole the empirical and descriptive studies as well as theoretical formulations from the fields of economics, political science, sociology, anthropology, and social psychology as they bear upon international development.

Again, these undertakings give far too little explicit attention to education, either in its broader or narrower sense, or to its dynamic role in international affairs, modernization, national planning, or economic and cultural development. Seldom are the results of social science research brought to bear upon educational policy, theory, or practice; seldom in turn is educational research used to illuminate the processes of social change.

I am happy to report that some significant gains are being made in this respect. With help from the Carnegie Corporation, the Harvard Graduate School of Education has set up a new Center for Studies in Education and Development; the University of Chicago Comparative Education Center has launched a series of research projects on education and socio-economic development in developing societies; the Institute of Advanced Projects of the East-West Center in Hawaii has given education high priority in its projected plans for research and study by scholars and fellows in international development; and a new Center for Comparative Education at Stanford will conduct research and train educational strategists to aid in the educational planning for developing nations.

Education has found a prominent place in the Office of Human Resources and Social Development of AID. I am assured that education will receive high priority in the plans of the new section on Research, Evaluation, and Planning Assistance which has been charged with contracting for research that will assist in improving the government's foreign assistance program. Meanwhile the Peace Corps has launched into the research field with enormous gusto. A conference held in Washington on March 4-5, 1963, on "The Behavioral Sciences and the Peace Corps" exhibited a range and vitality of research studies that are bound to have wide repercusions throughout the academic world and probably the length and breadth of international development. It took years to convince ICA/AID that research was necessary;

the Peace Corps apparently needed little persuading. I am sure that significant moves are being taken elsewhere as well, but the tasks are so great and so urgent that much more needs to be done.

The main point is clear: In fifteen years we have done much and we have learned much, but our experience and our studies need a vast amount of sifting and evaluation; and new programs of research should be launched to give sure-footed guidelines for building the future policies and activities of America's assistance role in international education. Social science centers should enlist the aid of professional educators on their staffs, and graduate schools of education should enlist the aid of social scientists on their staffs. All programs of technical assistance should have research study built in as a matter of course. Now that almost everyone has discovered on paper how important education is, we must get down to work to see what it has actually done and what it can do.

One purpose of research should be to analyze and appraise recent American educational programs as these have sought to aid other countries to improve their educational systems and processes. This research should be designed to describe and assess the educational practices, theories, and assumptions upon which our policies of international cooperation have been based, to discover and evaluate what has happened under varying conditions in different countries and regions of the world as a result of these policies, and to formulate principles that may guide the improvement of educational assistance policies in the future.

Particular attention should be given to projects sponsored by AID and the Peace Corps, but it would also be desirable to study the programs of voluntary agencies in order to gain a knowledge of comparable and contrasting theories and practices. This kind of policy research should seek basically to organize and extend the body of tested knowledge that will improve the theories and practices involved in American programs of assistance for the educational development of other countries. It should continue for periods long enough to validate the knowledge; for at least five years and, preferably, ten years.

Policy research should include analysis of the fundamental assumptions and operational practices of the AID and Peace Corps university contracts in education. We need to know precisely, for example, how effective have been the selection, orientation, training programs, and overseas performance of contract technicians and Peace Corps trainees. We should assess carefully the selection, training, and performance of the educational advisers of AID and the country representatives who have supervised Peace Corps teachers overseas. We should learn much more about the advantages and disadvantages of the training programs for students and educators from other countries who have come to America to study in the field of education and what happens to them upon their return home.

Underlying such practical questions of policy research in international education should be the continuing and long-range programs of empirical and theoretical research designed to develop warrantable generalizations concerning the fundamental role of education in the modernization process, national development, and social change. The most pervasive characteristic of recent times is the unparalleled extent and rate of change occurring among the various peoples and cultures of the world. As I have said earlier, the whole program of technical assistance itself is in essence a matter of deliberate education in social change, and every such program of social change involves the ideas, beliefs, customs, and education of the people involved, both senders and receivers.

In the long view, therefore, nothing could be more fundamentally important for the entire cooperative assistance enterprise than well conceived, well executed, independent programs of basic research on the direction, character, and prediction of social change as related to education. Basic research in the theory and practice of international education could be as important for designing technical assistance programs that will genuinely aid national development as basic research in the physical sciences is important for technological and developmental improvement in industry, government, space exploration, and national defense.

In order to deal with questions of policy as well as of fundamental social change the research should be interdisciplinary as well as international. The problems that face policy-makers as a result of social change cannot be limited to one field of activity nor to one field of knowledge. Each social science discipline has a special contribution to make in method or in substance. To marshal what is already known in a variety of social sciences and to conduct new research, scholars should be enlisted who are trained to see the relation of education to economics, political science, sociology, anthropology, social psychology, history, international relations, and comparative cultures.

In order to make better plans for the development of education in the economic, political, and social modernization of country X, research staffs would need to bring to bear what is already known about the direction in which the economy, government, and education of country X is moving, what is known about the dynamics of technological and social change in other countries at similar stages of development, and what happens educationally when new technology, new ideas, or new forms of social organization are introduced from one culture to another. Specific studies of the role of education in the political, economic, and sociological development of the particular country would be desirable. A large amount of rapidly growing knowledge in comparative education would need sifting, analysis, evaluation, and coordination.

Finally, new designs for research in country X would need to be drawn up to test what happens when various educational plans and policies are put into effect. Can we find short-cuts through the routes of urbanization, growth of literacy, and increased communication that have historically led to the modernization of traditional societies? Does the expansion of primary schools to extend literacy actually lead to increased per capita income? Can illiteracy be reduced as effectively by means of the "new technology" represented by learning machines, programed instruction, and mass media of communication as by training large numbers of primary school teachers? Do changes in curriculum content or pedagogical method have any noticeable effect upon the political, economical, or psychological development of a people? If more students are diverted to the sciences in the secondary schools, what happens to the standards of public administration as well as to the rate of industrialization? Does expanded opportunity for secondary education lead to greater social mobility or simply to greater unemployment among an educated elite? What happens if rural schools are expanded at the expense of urban schools, or technical studies at the expense of general studies, or universities at the expense of teacher training colleges? What happens to an educational aid program when a government "nationalizes" its schools? Does the introduction of American educational policies or practices into a dominantly French or British type of school or university system have good or ill effects? What are the relative advantages of multilateral as compared with bilateral educational aid programs? Does any change in curriculum or plan for education have much effect unless the examination system is changed?

Dozens of other research questions will come readily to mind for those who must make educational plans. Throughout the research enterprise the nationals of country X itself should be deeply involved in planning, gathering data, evaluating results, and formulating generalizations. Where necessary the training of nationals in research methods should be a prime objective of the assistance program.

Another type of basic research has to do with the way the dominant attitudes, behavior patterns, value systems, or personality characteristics of the people of country Y affect the development of education and the educational assistance programs. Relevant studies of nationalism and colonialism need to be brought to bear and evaluated. The new field of attitude research in modernizing areas, political behavior in international relations, stereotypes and images of foreigners, nonverbal communication patterns, and international communication may have relevance.

Building upon what is already known, special research could then be carried forward to see what role education does play and can play in creating and changing the images that the people of country Y hold of other peoples. Meanwhile, long-range studies of the way personal outlooks, interpersonal relations, and national attitudes are generated and changed and the role education plays therein should be pursued. We should continue to study the personal, social, and intellectual characteristics required by Americans in successful cross-cultural contact and international cooperation. Much more sensitive and difficult but equally important would be studies of what kind of personal and professional characteristics make host-country nationals effective or ineffective as they take part in the educational assistance transaction.

In all this we should be alert to develop a new breed of development educators knowledgeable in international studies, skilled in the arts of educational assistance, and devoted to the tasks of educational planning and development in modernizing nations. Their study of the international aspects of education, economics, politics, sociology, anthropology, and psychology should enable them to relate educational planning to the over-all national development of technology, industry, agriculture, political organization, and health and welfare services. Their task is to focus on the function of education in the total effort to improve the conditions of life in a rapidly developing society and in the total process by which people are motivated to help themselves through community, national, and international action.

Too often formal education has been neglected in this task. Professional educators and social scientists often look upon "education" simply as a formal school matter unrelated to the fundamental changes going on in a country's industry, agriculture, public administration, or health services. On the contrary, "education" should be viewed as including informal, community, and adult education as well as that which goes on inside schools and universities. Technical assistance programs will be improved, and education in both its formal and informal senses will make a greater contribution if they are seen as integral parts of a total enterprise of international development. We not only need greater attention to the part that education can and must play in international development; we also need much more explicit recognition and study of the educational role of technical assistance itself.

So far the research on technical assistance has been far too spotty and inadequate, but the training programs for overseas educational advisers have been even more spotty or nonexistent—with but a few notable exceptions. Part of the difficulty has been the excessive speed with which technicians have been sent overseas, often after interminable delays in arriving at the decision to send them at all. Part of the difficulty, too, has been the lack of conviction on the part of some ICA/AID officials and some congressmen that training is necessary or represents a legitimate use of funds. But even when these elements are not present, it has been difficult to gather enough people together who are going to a particular country at the same time to warrant mounting a full-scale training program for them.

In this respect, the new projects for sending large numbers of teachers and Peace Corps volunteers overseas have great advantage over the classic technical assistance approach. Training programs for this new stage in American international education have been able to profit from shortcomings revealed in technical assistance projects. In return, revitalized educational assistance programs can now take place if they will draw upon the accumulations of international knowledge that are being developed in university centers of social science research, if professional educators can play a larger and more central role in the preparation of the American and foreign participants, and if something of the youthful eagerness, service motivation, and lively intelligence of the young overseas teachers can be injected into the endeavors of the more mature overseas professors.

When the intellectual and scholarly resources of the new international studies are teamed up on one side with the skills and wisdom of highly trained technical assistance advisers and harnessed on the other side with the educational arts of a large corps of qualified American teachers, not only will the image of America abroad be radically changed but the countries concerned will have available for their national development the best combination of America's educational talents. America's troika in the race for international educational assistance will be unbeatable.

✾ 3 ✾

Overseas Teachers:
Helping Hands for Rising Nations

Until late in the 1950s it looked as though America's role in international education would settle down to the two major endeavors already described; namely, a deepened interest in international studies and an educational component in technical assistance. But the years straddling 1960 proved to be a significant turning point. On one hand, scholarly studies in economics and politics began to stress the importance of "human resources," as well as monetary and physical resources in the development of the emerging nations; basic to this development of human resources is education.

On the other hand, new nations began to "emerge" faster than most people had expected: forty-nine in twenty years. In the nine years between 1943 and 1951 sixteen new nations became independent, most of them in Asia. In the three years from 1956 to 1958 six more became independent, five of them in Africa; and in the three years of 1960, 1961, and 1962, twenty-seven achieved independence, all but four in Africa. This process of nation-founding, whereby nearly half of all the nations in the world today are less than twenty years old in political independence, is one of the astonishing phenomena of modern times. Nearly all of them want more and better education—as do the older but still underdeveloped nations of Latin America. Requests for educational assistance from the economically developed countries have mushroomed beyond all expectations, and the educa-

48

tional policies formulated in the earlier days of technical assistance were no longer adequate to meet the demand of rising educational expectations.

As the march to independence took place the economists' generalizations took on an insistent reality that could no longer be denied. The highest priority for countries that were just beginning the transition from traditional to modern forms of society was the development of their human resources. In countries where literacy rates are less than 10 to 25 per cent, where only 15 to 25 per cent of the primary school age group is actually in school, where only 2 to 3 per cent of the secondary school age group goes to school, and where only 1– or 2–10ths of 1 per cent of the university age group attends higher institutions, it was clear that there were too few trained people to man the governmental, administrative, technical, and professional positions required of a modern independent nation. In these cases it has become equally clear that the building of human resources through education and training must come before money, capital investment, or even technical advice can do a great deal of good in attacking frontally the problems of modernization.

Above all, it is clear that countries entering the transitional stage of modernization need teachers more than they need any other kind of educational assistance from the outside. They cannot maintain the educational institutions they already have simply by being given or loaned more money; they need teachers who will help to get their children through secondary schools in sufficient numbers to produce those who can become the teachers of the future. They cannot build new educational institutions simply with advice from high level technical advisers or with money for new buildings; they need qualified teachers in expanding numbers, first from the outside, and eventually from their own teacher training institutions—which in turn also need teachers. The demands for trained personnel in some newly independent nations of Africa are so great that the qualified teachers they do have are likely to be drawn off to administrative or governmental posts, thus making the shortage of teachers even more acute.

But they must have teachers to help them train a larger cadre of educated people from whom they can draw administrators, managers, planners, professionals, and still more teachers. To achieve this, they need above all to borrow teachers temporarily from other countries for their secondary schools and higher institutions. They need outside help to man the schools and universities they have and the ones they want to build. They need thousands of "expatriates" from overseas to enter their schools and engage in direct educational service for them. Similarly, it is estimated that English-speaking universities in Africa alone will need 5,000 expatriate teachers in the next fifteen years, most of whom will have to come from the United States.[1] In our efforts at international education America has come only lately to realize what the least developed nations need most; namely, teachers.

When this was realized, the American government began to respond on a large and organized scale in early 1961. It was this situation that led ICA to ask Teachers College to recruit, select, and train candidates for the Teachers for East Africa project in January 1961. It was this situation that the Peace Corps found so demanding after it was established by the President in March 1961. These programs began with different assumptions and developed along somewhat different lines, but they both represented a break with the foreign aid philosophy that all technical assistance, even in education, had somehow to be justified as a direct means or tool of purely economic development. It was now recognized that educational assistance need not be solely in the form of technical advice and consultation as offered by "high-level" outside experts but could also take the form

[1] See the summary of the UNESCO conference on the development of higher education in Africa held at Tananarive in September 1962, written by A. M. Carr-Saunders, *Staffing African Universities* (London: Overseas Development Institute, 1963). Voluntary, non-governmental efforts in the United States to meet such needs as these on a long-term basis have led to plans for the organization of a new agency to be called Overseas Educational Service (OES), not yet publicly announced at the time of writing. Closely related to Education and World Affairs, OES will stimulate the recruitment and selection of able American faculty members for foreign universities and will aid in the establishment of conditions of service that will enable well-established professors to accept relatively long overseas assignments with the assurance that the future in their home institutions will not be jeopardized during their absence with respect to salary, status, retirement, and other benefits.

of actual service for the receiving nation by regular teachers who were employed to work within the organizational structure of the country concerned.

By the end of 1963 Teachers College had sent more than 400 teachers to East Africa, and the Peace Corps planned to have some 5,000 teachers in many parts of the world; all in less than three years.

TEACHERS FOR EAST AFRICA

A distinctive characteristic of the Teachers for East Africa project (TEA) is that it combines the supply of teachers for educational service overseas with technical assistance designed to help increase the number of qualified teachers who will be trained within East Africa. The supply of qualified expatriate teachers can therefore be planned and coordinated with the development and training of qualified African teachers. The project does not simply stand to one side and advise, nor does it rush in to set up separate institutions parallel to those already existing. It does not try to export kits of American educational practices or neatly tied-up curriculum packages.

It does try to supply fully qualified teachers who will fit into the system that now exists, who will serve the host country not only by working within it but by working for it. If and when the time comes that the country wishes to adapt its education to its own newly perceived needs, the teachers will be there as knowledgeable and experienced professionals to respond to the request to work at the problem of designing an education that is not British, not American, but East African.

Let me try to recapture something of the spirit of TEA by quoting a few paragraphs from a welcoming speech I gave to the first group of TEA teachers at the opening session of their orientation program at Teachers College on June 26, 1961:

I think that the real significance of our gathering here is that we are creating a college. . . . If we are successful in this venture, it will be because we have been successful in forming ourselves into a college in its most elemental sense, i.e., a group of persons engaged together in the common pursuit of knowledge and of understanding with a view to the enhancement of life for others.

Our college will be new in two respects: First, we will together seek not only to know and to understand as all colleges do but to teach others to know and to understand. We shall be forming a *teaching college* (not a teachers college in any usual sense, but a teaching college). Secondly, our locale is not simply Morningside Heights in New York, nor Blooms- bury in London, nor Makerere Hill in Kampala, but it embraces the schools and people of East Africa as well, and thus it touches the world.

What we are about to do is to make explicit what is really the task of every liberal or general college. A college should not only teach its stu- dents something of value for themselves and then stop there; it should expect and enable its students to teach that something to others and to do it for the benefit of the others, not solely for the benefit of themselves. Unless a college attempts to become a teaching college it may really be only a trade school or a technical institute, training people to do a specific job designed to earn a living for themselves. This is of course very impor- tant, but if it fully lives up to its mission, a college should be the vehicle of extending its knowledge and its understanding to an ever-widening circle through the teaching its graduates carry on throughout their lives. In some careers the teaching function may be in the background; in our careers it is the foreground as well.

Recognizing that TEA was an experimental and pilot project, we tried to impart to it six general characteristics which we believed to be the marks of any good overseas educational operation:

1. *The program is based upon a genuine and demonstrable need in the receiving country.*

I believe that this has been well documented in our case. East Africa desperately needs secondary school teachers. Members of the African Liaison Committee of the American Council on Education (all well-known college presidents) who traveled throughout East Africa in the summer of 1960 were convinced of the need for second- ary school teachers to be supplied from outside. Subsequent to their visit in East Africa a conference was held at Princeton, New Jersey in December 1960 to consider the educational problems of British East Africa—Kenya, Tanganyika, Uganda, and Zanzibar. The conference was supported by the Carnegie Corporation of New York. The participants included representatives of government, education, and voluntary agencies of the territories named as well as similar representatives from the United Kingdom and the United States. The roster of those present was a multinational Who's Who of persons knowledgeable about East African education.

The spokesmen for the African governments—soon to become fully independent—reported that their most pressing need was the expansion of secondary education and that the greatest obstacle to meeting that need was the shortage of qualified teachers for their secondary schools.

A proposal was put forward that the United States help to alleviate this shortage by selecting 150 American teachers to go to East Africa and teach in the secondary schools for two years. The idea was endorsed and become the leading recommendation of the Princeton conference report. TEA therefore grew directly out of the combined efforts of academic and professional groups working closely with responsible government officials and with representatives of private agencies and institutions of higher education. There were few if any political overtones.

Immediately following the conference there was much activity in many places: in the International Cooperation Administration in Washington; in the ministries of education in Kenya, Tanganyika, Uganda, and Zanzibar; in the British Colonial Office in London; at Makerere College in Kampala, Uganda; and in the offices of the Afro-Anglo-American Program in Teacher Education at Teachers College whose executive officer, Professor Karl W. Bigelow, was at the center of the preliminary planning.

With unprecedented speed ICA arranged for Teachers College to take major professional responsibility for the American end of the plan. It was expected that a number of graduates from British universities would also join in the scheme. This would make it doubly an international venture, a foretaste, we hoped, of other multinational efforts. As a matter of fact, eight British teachers joined the first year; nearly fifty the second year; and the plans were for an equal number of Americans and British the third year, approximately 140 each.

The administration of the project was put into my hands, and within a few days of the ICA request I went to London and to East Africa in February 1961 accompanied by two Columbia University colleagues and two representatives of ICA. As a result of our visit the plan for the first year turned out to be as follows:

The 150 Americans selected for the program comprised the following three groups:

(a) Group A consisted of about sixty teachers who held at least a bachelor's degree, were professionally trained and certified, and had had some experience in secondary school teaching;

(b) Group B consisted of about forty recent arts and science graduates who had a bachelor's degree but no professional preparation for teaching; and

(c) Group C consisted of about fifty recent graduates who had at least a bachelor's degree and who had finished their professional preparation for teaching in secondary schools but who had had no teaching experience beyond practice teaching.

All participants in the program received a short period of orientation at Teachers College beginning June 26, 1961 and further training within East Africa appropriate to their respective academic and professional backgrounds.

Group A, the experienced teachers, went to Makerere College on July 15 for about two months of training before being assigned to a teaching post in a secondary school beginning in August 1961.

Group B went to Makerere College on July 15 for an academic year's training before being assigned to a teaching post in May 1962. The eight British graduates joined the program for Group B at this point. Their course of training culminated in the award of the Makerere Diploma in Education, and thus they met the full requirements for professionally qualified teachers in East African secondary schools. Indeed, it was substantially the same qualification required of teachers in the United Kingdom and other Commonwealth nations.

Group C remained at Teachers College for the summer session of 1961 and then received further orientation at the University of London Institute of Education during September. After completing this course, Group C went to Makerere College about the first of October for three months of further training before being assigned to teaching posts in January 1962.

Upon selection for the program each person received an East Africa Training Fellowship for the period of orientation and training at Teachers College, at Makerere College, and at the University of London. They were specifically selected to meet three requirements: to fill vacancies in the schools that could not be otherwise filled by qualified teachers (as designated in detail by each government), to teach the subject fields in which there were the greatest shortages, and to meet the requests for posts to be filled by men or by women teachers. Men outnumbered women about 3 to 1. The need for teachers of mathematics and science was greatest, followed by English, history, and geography.

2. *The program is based upon cooperative planning and careful preparation in the receiving countries.*

Demonstration of need is not the sole characteristic of a good program of international educational service. The host country must also genuinely desire assistance for specific, well-defined, and limited purposes that are carefully worked out.

During our first visit to East Africa my colleagues and I talked with the highest government officials, with territorial and provincial education officers, with faculty members and administrators of Makerere College, and with headmasters and teachers in the secondary schools. We spent time in the cities and in the bush. We saw politicians, civil servants, officials of teachers' associations, business and labor organizations, and ordinary working people. We conferred with Africans, Asians, Europeans, and Americans.

We worked long hours with responsible educational, governmental, and financial authorities in each of the territorial governments and in the United Kingdom. We arrived at carefully worked out and detailed arrangements for the training and the subsequent service of the American teachers in the government schools and government-aided secondary schools of East Africa.

We were struck by the unanimous and genuine enthusiasm for the plan as expressed in every quarter of East African life. Nothing was viewed as more urgent than the filling of vacancies with qualified teachers. The scheme was welcomed wholeheartedly by all shades of opinion.

We returned to London and the United States with signed agreements whereby each government undertook to employ the American teachers and pay them at the same rate as its own teachers are paid. Willingness to expend its own money is a good sign that the receiving country not only needs but wants such assistance.

In October-December of 1961, my colleagues and I were again in East Africa and met with officials to plan the second contingent of teachers to be selected in 1962; and, as I have indicated in the preface to this book, we have recently returned from a third trip during which the conference at Entebbe in January 1963 worked out detailed proposals for the third contingent to be selected and trained in 1963. Continuous planning and consultation by the officials of the governments and universities involved is a prime requirement if academic and professional goals are to be achieved along with the broadly developmental goals.

3. *The teachers are carefully recruited, screened, and selected.*

On this score we sought counsel and assistance from many sources qualified in international education, but we turned first of all to the American colleges and universities themselves. Each year I sent letters to the presidents and deans of all accredited, four-year, degree-granting institutions that offer basic work in the arts, sciences, and education. I asked these officials to assist us in finding and selecting topnotch students or recent graduates who would be qualified, who would be interested, and who would therefore come with the highest recommendations for such a venture. Subsequent screening based upon academic records, recommendations of qualified referees, personal interviews, tests, and medical examinations was undertaken by the selection board at Teachers College. We sent several interviewing teams to different parts of the country. The interviewers, selected from a score of colleges and universities, were knowledgeable about Africa, about teaching, and about American college and university students.

What kind of person were we looking for?

We wanted first-rate teachers who were well-trained in the academic subjects regularly taught in the East African secondary schools.

We wanted them to be fully qualified professionally, or capable of becoming so through the training that was provided for them.

We wanted teachers who were personally versatile, resourceful, and imaginative in surmounting the unexpected, the difficult, or the merely routine. They should be able to rely upon their own inner resources rather than upon others. They should have a moral integrity to guide them when rules are strangely different or when customary rules are removed.

We wanted those who would be capable of relating themselves readily to new situations, new associates, new friends. With no trace of paternalism they should be able to cooperate with Africa in educating itself.

They should be animated by a spirit of service that is realistic not sentimental, by a spirit of adventure that is durable not romantic, by a sense of altruism that stems from a fraternal concern for the welfare of others not from the posture of superior "do-goodism" for the unfortunate. Their spirit of public service should carry no hint of proselyting on behalf of partisan politics or sectarian religion.

They should be knowledgeable about American life and education and ready to learn understandingly about the people and cultures of other lands. They should exemplify the free man and his values, not the aggressive preacher of slogans or pat phrases.

4. *The teachers are specially trained for their task, and substantial training is given in the host country prior to employment.*

Sound motivation and high quality are essential for international teaching service, but they alone are not sufficient. Good orientation and training are also essential. We provided varying lengths of time for orientation at Teachers College, for training at Makerere College, and for orientation by the ministries of education of the host countries.

In the second year we made some changes in the training programs, principally by shortening the over-all programs for groups A and C; namely, those who had already had professional training. They were given five to six weeks' training at Teachers College, but they were not sent to Makerere. Members of Group A (experienced teachers) went directly to their countries of assignment for two weeks of orientation by the respective ministries of education. Members of Group C (qualified but inexperienced teachers) were given an eight weeks' cadetship or internship in the schools of their assignment before taking over full teaching duties. The eight months' diploma course at Makerere for Group B (the untrained liberal arts graduates who are comparable to most Peace Corps volunteers) was not shortened, but it was modified in important respects. Some feel it is still too long and not tailored sufficiently to the needs of American and British graduates. But the ministries of education in the East African governments preferred that the full course and full requirements for professional qualification be met by the expatriate teachers; thus the full Makerere program was retained for the third year of the program.

In general, the training programs have stressed five elements:

(a) An over-all orientation to Africa, its politics, culture, aspirations, and present role in the world; and a fundamental study of the geography, history, social anthropology, economics, and politics of the countries of East Africa;

(b) an introduction to the British system of education which is the prototype of East African secondary education as it now exists; and a special study of East African education, its history and current trends, and the national policies of governmental and educational administration;

(c) specific training and practice in teaching the content of the subjects required by East African school conditions, syllabuses, and examination requirements, and aid in facing the problem of teaching in English which is the medium of instruction of the schools but essentially a foreign language for the students;

(d) a re-examination of various aspects of American life and education as they may be useful to the American teacher as he deals with African students and British and African colleagues and as he gains new perspectives on himself and his own culture; and

(e) an opportunity to learn Swahili, the most common spoken language of the region, as a means of enhancing and supplementing the communication achieved by the use of English in the classroom.

Table I. ATTRITION IN TEA PROJECT
(June 1961 to June 1963)

	Number Entering Training at Teachers College	Terminated during Training in United States	Departed for Overseas	Terminated during Training in East Africa	Terminated after Assignment to Schools	Total Number Terminated
Group A-I	64	2	July 1961	0	5	7
Group B-I	39	0	July 1961	1	0	1
Group C-I	54	1	Sept. 1961	2	1	4
Group A-II	35	1	Aug. 1962	0	1	2
Group B-II	47	0	July 1962	7	0	7
Group C-II	33	0	Oct. 1962	0	1	1
TOTAL	272	4 (1.5%)		10 (3.7%)	8 (2.9%)	22 (8.1%)

For Group B most of the training was done in East Africa itself with much opportunity for firsthand acquaintance with East African life and eight weeks of teaching practice in the schools, as well as substantive study of the job to be done. How much of such training and what kind is most useful for Americans of differing experience and background is still a matter for careful scrutiny and judgment in the TEA program.

In general, however, we have been highly gratified at the results of our selection procedures and training programs. As in most fellowship programs based upon careful selection procedures, we have assumed that once the trainees were selected they would remain in the program unless something happened to change our minds during the training. Between June 1961 and June 1963 there were 272 teachers selected who reported to Teachers College for training. Of these a total of 22 (8.1 per cent) left the program: four (1.5 per cent) resigned or were asked to withdraw while in training in New York; another ten (3.7 per cent) resigned or were asked to withdraw during training in East Africa. This is a total of 5.2 per cent casualties during training. In addition, there were eight (2.9 per cent) who resigned after assignment to the schools: one for reasons of health, one wife who became pregnant, and one couple whose husband was asked to join the TEA staff at Makerere. This meant that only four (1.5 per cent) resigned for reasons that could fairly be classified as "not having worked out well in the schools." (See Table I on p. 59.)

I do not know what the exact comparable figures for the Peace Corps' much larger training programs may be. Comparison is difficult, because the Peace Corps recruits for a wide variety of non-teaching projects in many different countries, and its policy is to rely heavily upon the training programs as part of the selective process. This means that as many as 30 per cent have been "selected out" of some training programs with the termination rate for all training programs being 15.9 per cent for two years.

As of June 30, 1963 the Peace Corps reported that 289 volunteers out of 4,855 sent overseas had been returned: 63 for "compassionate" reasons, 183 for "adjustment" reasons, 37 for medical reasons, and 6 deceased. This amounts to 5.9 per cent of all those sent overseas after training; and presumedly about 4 per cent of all returnees came home for reasons that could fairly be included under the heading "They did not work out well." Apparently, there is some difference in "mortality on the job" between TEA and Peace Corps at large. Accurate comparisons with TEA would, however, need to be confined to Peace Corps secondary school teaching projects in Africa where the conditions are somewhat similar to those in East Africa. The tables on pp. 62–63 make a start at such comparisons.

Between July 1961 and September 1962, the Peace Corps had seven training programs for sending secondary school teachers to West Africa in countries where the medium of instruction is in English, where the requirements for teachers' qualifications are high, and where the schools have generally followed a British standard of secondary education based upon an external examination system. Therefore, the comparison has been made between TEA and those Peace Corps projects in Ghana, Nigeria, and Sierra Leone in which the teachers had been overseas for six months or longer by June 1963. (See Tables I, II, and III).

Some of the interesting differences are as follows: The percentage of total terminations after entering training is approximately three times as great in the Peace Corps as in TEA. The percentage of terminations during training in the United States is roughly ten times as high in the Peace Corps as in TEA, but if the total training period is considered by adding the training in Africa to the training in the United States, the Peace Corps terminations during training are again three times that of TEA. If, however, the number of terminations after departure for overseas is considered alone, then the percentage for TEA is slightly more than that of the Peace Corps. The percentage of terminations after assignment to schools is twice as high for the Peace Corps as for TEA.

These preliminary comparisons will serve to raise questions concerning the different approaches being taken to selection procedures, the use of training as a selection device and as a means of building motivation for professional service, and the value of reliance upon overseas training as part of the total training process. They say nothing as yet concerning relative effectiveness of performance of the job to be done in the schools or the ability to adjust to life and service in another culture. The debate on those subjects has scarcely begun.

5. *The teachers are carefully inducted and supervised by professionals in the host country.*

Table II. ATTRITION IN SEVEN PEACE CORPS SECONDARY EDUCATION
PROJECTS IN WEST AFRICA
(*July 1961 to June 1963*)

	Training Institution	Number Entering Training	Terminated during Training in United States	Departed for Overseas	Terminated after Assignment to Schools Overseas	Total Number Terminated
Ghana I	U. of Calif. (Berkeley)	59	7	Aug. 1961	6	13
Nigeria I	Harvard	46	9	Sept. 1961	4	13
Nigeria III	U. of Calif. (Los Angeles)	52	10	Dec. 1961	5	15
Sierra Leone I	Teachers College Columbia U.	57	20	Jan. 1962	1	21
Ghana II	U. of Calif. (Berkeley)	60	11	Aug. 1962	2	13
Sierra Leone II	State Univ. of N.Y. (New Paltz)	61	5	Sept. 1962	6	11
Nigeria IV	U. of Calif. (Los Angeles)	90	9	Sept. 1962	2	11
TOTAL		425	71 (16.7%)		26 (6.1%)	97 (22.8%)

We are convinced that professional supervision for the untrained
and inexperienced teachers is indispensable. It was fortunate, therefore,
that Teachers College and Makerere College were not strangers to
one another. Makerere is one of the eight African institutions of
teacher education that are cooperating with the University of London
Institute of Education and with Teachers College in the Afro-Anglo-
American Program in Teacher Education supported by the Carnegie
Corporation. This association has meant that we were able to engage

Table III. Comparison of Attrition Rates Between TEA
and Peace Corps Secondary Education Projects in West Africa*
(*Entered training between June 1961 and September 1962;
overseas for at least six months*)

	TEA (As of June 30, 1963)	Per Cent of Total	Peace Corps (As of June 30, 1963)	Per Cent of Total
Number entering training in U.S.A.	272		425	
Terminated during training in U.S.A.	4	1.5	71	16.7
Terminated during training in Africa	10	3.7		
Terminated after assignment to schools	8	2.9	26	6.1
Total terminated after entering training	22	8.1	97	22.8

* Source of Peace Corps figures is *The Peace Corps Volunteer: a Quarterly Statistical Summary,* Division of Volunteer Support, Peace Corps, Washington, D.C., June 30, 1963. The projects included here are identified as Ghana I, Ghana II, Nigeria I, Nigeria III, Nigeria IV, Sierra Leone I, and Sierra Leone II.

in a good deal of face-to-face planning in the early stages of the project.

Staff cooperation has taken several forms. Members of the Makerere and London staffs have come to Teachers College to aid in the orientation of the teachers. The plan from the beginning has included sending American faculty members appointed by Teachers College to be assigned to the Makerere faculty of Education to assist as needed to meet the increased teaching demands occasioned by the influx of large numbers of American and British graduate students. Alongside their Makerere colleagues they have taught classes and supervised the teaching practice of African, Asian, and European as well as American students. They have assisted the Makerere staff in the informal follow-up of the American teachers after they were on the job in the schools, just as the Makerere staff does for all its former students. And they have taken part in revisions of the Makerere program of courses, syllabuses, and even the instituting of a new bachelor's degree in education (B.Ed.), a type of innovation that is being tried in several African institutions for the first time.

Once training has been completed and the American teachers have been employed by the East African governments, the American teachers are considered to be regular government education officers, responsible to the same officials, receiving the same pay, undergoing the same conditions of service, and living in the same way as other expatriate teachers. The East African governments pay the same base salary to the expatriate teachers that they pay their own teachers; and the British and American governments pay a modest overseas addition to their respective nationals. In other words, the salaries and conditions of service of the American teachers are defined by the governments concerned with respect to the qualifications, status, training, and salary required for effective accomplishment of the job to be done. Sharing in the cost of salaries by all the governments concerned makes the enterprise a truly cooperative and multilateral affair.

The task of the TEA teachers has been to fill vacancies for which no other qualified teacher, African or expatriate, was available. They took no job that an African could fill. In fact their ultimate goal is to assist Africa in expanding and developing secondary education and the training of teachers in such a way that East Africa can most rapidly move to supply its own teachers. The principle of Africanization is fully accepted. It is fully recognized that the role of the African governments in educational development will increase in the years ahead under independence and self-government.

6. *The quality of the program is carefully assessed at every stage.*

From the beginning we tried to be constantly alert to test the assumptions upon which the program is built and to evaluate the decisions made. The TEA program is exceptionally well suited for reseach. The three different groups of trainees representing different types of education and background can be subjected to careful observation.

Eventually, we ought to be able to answer such questions as these:

Was the selection really well done? What kind of person succeeds? or fails? Does the recent arts or science graduate do as well as the graduate with professional training? Does the untrained graduate need nine months of training or can he get along with nine weeks? Is the experienced American teacher more versatile or less versatile in East African schools than is his inexperienced colleague? Is the Makerere Diploma in Education course designed on British models for African graduates a suitable way to prepare American and British graduates for teaching in East Africa, or is professional training in the United States or in Britain just as suitable? Is practice teaching in the United States for American teachers as useful as practice teaching in the host country? How good are personality tests, interviews, academic records, and written references as predictors of success? How can screening, selecting, orienting, and training be improved? How do the Americans compare with their African, Asian, or European colleagues? Do experienced American teachers need the longer and more intensive training they have received as compared with the experienced British teacher? What kinds of secondary education and teacher training are most suitable for a nation that seeks not only to be independent but to be genuinely self-governing and free? What kinds of changes in East African education are taking place as a result of the presence of TEA teachers?

Fortunately, AID was persuaded to permit a small amount of research funds to be included in the TEA contract, so I am hoping that we shall eventually have some answers to questions such as those mentioned above. They are so important, however, for educational improvement in America and Britain as well as in all developing countries that a much larger research effort should be undertaken.

The American teachers in East Africa will need to fit into a British system of education where the students presently see their main goal as passing the external examinations and obtaining the school certificate which acts as a passport to higher education or to a preferred job. The American teachers will thus need to be fully competent in the teaching of systematic and orderly knowledge, in keeping standards high, and in thoroughness of mastery and workmanship. If they fail at the traditional task of academic scholarship, they will fail utterly.

At the same time, they have been plunged into societies that are undergoing rapid change. Tanganyika achieved independence during the first year after our teachers arrived in East Africa; Uganda during the second year; and Kenya and Zanzibar during the third year. The teachers may thus be called upon to see ways to expand and adapt education to meet the growing demands for self-government and to assist in designing an education appropriate to the achievement of genuine freedom once independence has been won.

The accelerated pace of social change in East Africa will call for all the qualities of versatility, innovation, flexibility, expansiveness, and humanitarianism that marked educational progressivism at its best. The American teacher must be equally adept at the tasks of academic scholarship and of educational innovation. Can he do as well as British teachers have done in promoting academic scholarship? Can he put the qualities of American education (qualities that have given it both substance and vitality) at the disposal of other countries in such a way as to meet their needs and not impose his system upon them? This is a most delicate and challenging task.

Fortunately, I had a chance to gain some firsthand impressions concerning the way the original hopes and plans for TEA are working out through visits and talks with 52 of the first 62 American teachers to be assigned to the schools. True, these were all experienced teachers and they had only been in their schools for a few months. The "honeymoon" period was still on, but nevertheless I believe my impressions are worth reporting, and I would not be surprised if the research findings eventually substantiate many of these first impressions.

In the course of my visits to the schools in late 1961, I observed the teachers at work in their classrooms and on the school grounds, as well as in the community. I interviewed the teachers, of course; but I also talked with their headmasters and colleagues on the school staffs, their students, people in their communities, and right up the administrative line from district education officers, to permanent secretaries and ministers of education. I had the pleasure of seeing the Prime Minister of Tanganyika, Julius K. Nyerere, now president of the republic, on two different occasions. From all these sources I gained a number of general impressions.

There are some problems, of course, but my over-all impression was that most of the teachers were doing very well indeed and that there were fewer problems of settling-in and of adjustment than sixty well qualified American teachers would have had if they had been appointed to forty new and different schools in the United States at the beginning of a new term.

The second basic impression I gained was that there were fewer major difficulties in the realm of teaching or academic preparation than we had expected. There had been a good deal of doubt expressed as to whether the academic preparation of the American teachers and their ability to teach in a different setting would measure up to accepted standards. By and large, I found no real problem on this score. A far greater problem arises when the teachers are asked to teach subjects for which they are not prepared. Where real academic difficulties have arisen, they lie in this quarter.

With respect to relationships with students, the general report was that the students seemed to respond well to the American teachers. This was substantiated by my own personal observations inside and outside the classroom. There is something about being new and different. Whether it is being new and different, or whether it is being American or whether it is both I cannot tell. But there did seem to be a healthy kind of student responsiveness in most of the schools I visited.

In general, American teachers as a group have entered into the life of African schools with an enthusiasm and energy which is a matter of remark by headmasters and by staff. This is true even though most of them were not accustomed to the round-the-clock demands of boarding school life. They are coaching debating teams, directing plays, starting magazines, and sponsoring correspondence between their African students and their former students at the schools they have left back home. They are engaging in sports with a zest that

some schools had not seen before. From climbing mountains to preparing biological specimens in the laboratory, they seemed to be getting on well with their students.

Relationships in the community were generally also very good.
There were, however, some problems relating to the joining of sports
clubs, or social clubs. In some of the communities there may be only
one club, and it has traditionally been open only to "Europeans."
When all the "Europeans" in the club are British, the interesting
question arises as to whether or not an American is a "European,"
but it raises the still more awkward question when the American is a
Negro. Is an American Negro a "European"? There have been some
touchy problems on this score, especially as the countries gained their
independence and the question of segregated clubs became an open
and public issue. My guess is that the presence of American teachers,
white and Negro alike, will aid the transition to nonsegregated social
clubs.

However, the most common problem the American teachers reported with respect to their school life was their relationship with the
British and the African staff. The Americans generally were not quite
prepared for the reserve, the aloofness, or the formality of some of
the older British teachers. By "older" I do not necessarily mean old
in age, but the type of master whose caustic tongue in the common
room gave the impression that he was not only aloof but somehow
felt himself to be superior to the brash newcomers.

Many of the American teachers were not prepared for this attitude,
and they sometimes reacted negatively and aggressively. They may
think of themselves as going into a strange setting as Americans with
an open, friendly, good feeling toward everyone and, if anything, with
pro-African sympathies. In a few cases I am fairly sure that some of
the American teachers deliberately overplayed friendliness to African
students, staff, and community to show their contempt for what they
deemed an arrogant British attitude. And in some cases I think the
British suspected and resented this.

However, the more I probed this point the more I discovered that
there is not a single British attitude toward Americans any more than

there is a single American or African attitude. Time and again, an American teacher would report with enthusiasm the recent arrival from Britain of a teacher with whom he could work very well indeed. In other words, there are older types and newer types of British expatriate teachers just as there are different types of American and African teachers. The older "colonial" school-master type has a stiffly formal attitude toward his colleagues and his students of whatever race or nationality, and the newer type has roughly the same motivation of service and concern for his students that the good teacher anywhere has. They get on admirably together.

There has also been some surprise expressed by the American teachers that the African staff members have often been quite reserved and apparently reluctant to respond cordially and easily to the Americans' open-armed, fresh, friendly attitude. The Americans have been surprised to find how formal and reserved in manner are many East African teachers, not realizing that this has been long cultivated by their own traditional customs as well as by the British educational system. Indeed, some African teachers may at first be somewhat doubtful, not to say suspicious, of the American's motivation in being there at all.

On the whole, the American teachers are conducting themselves admirably. They are self-sufficient, they are making do cheerfully where they need to make do, and in some cases, I am convinced, they are acting as go-betweens in bridging racial distance or even healing ruptures that have had long standing in some schools.

Finally, several types of criticism have been leveled at American teachers by their British headmasters and colleagues. The first has to do with their use of the English language—not their accents—but their pronunciation, their spelling, and their "Americanisms" in English usage. This subject was a matter of jocularity on many occasions; but sometimes it was tinged with more acid than humor, especially when the American usage or speech was slovenly and careless. "American" English can seldom compete successfully with "English" English in such circumstances. So those Americans who teach English and those who use English should be prepared for occasional caustic remarks about their Americanisms—from Africans as well as from Britons.

A second item that caused a good deal of adverse comment concerning some of the American men teachers was their general appearance, their dress—and their scraggly beards. Some of this comment reflects a higher regard by the African and British teacher for formality in personal conduct and for the status of secondary school teachers than is customary among Americans. The occasion even arose, especially where a headmaster was particularly concerned about the "standard of dress," when it seemed that some of the Americans took special delight in wearing what to them may have been acceptable on an American college campus but what must have appeared to the Britons and to the Africans alike to be disheveled and unkempt garb.

In some degree these differences reflect fairly deep cultural differences between educated Americans and educated Britons with regard to the importance of formality, manners, and friendliness. What an American from the rural Mid-West may regard as perfectly natural friendliness may be regarded by Britons or Africans as rude or aggressively irritating behavior. An American's "natural" informality with students in class or with servants at home may be regarded by his British or African colleagues as seriously undermining the discipline or authority rightfully due to a teacher, a headmaster, or an educated employer. The freedom of behavior an American parent might easily allow his children at home or at school may be taken as the rankest kind of abdication of parental obligation. American egalitarian behavior which comes naturally at home may become exaggerated abroad when confronted by social class distinctions that have in turn seemed quite natural to colonial Britons and to British-educated Africans. To a British master, the American teacher's zeal for hard and long hours of work and play is somehow unbecoming in an intellectual; to an American teacher who feels he has only two years to do the job, the leisurely British pace and long vacations somehow seem to add up to an indifference and apathy toward the urgent need for education in Africa.

Let me conclude this part with a summary of some of the most important contributions that I believe TEA is making to education in East Africa:

1. The immediate emergency in shortage of teachers is being met. For the first time within the memory of some headmasters the schools are reasonably well staffed, thanks to the presence of TEA teachers. This removes a kind of chronic irritation and disability from the schools. This is a tremendous achievement.

2. The presence of TEA teachers means that the development plans for the expansion of secondary education are also being made possible. The several countries are in the midst of crash programs for the expansion of secondary education which could not take place without a supply of expatriate teachers. For example, Tanganyika is trying to make it possible for every boy or girl who enters secondary school to stay the four years and have a chance at the school certificate examinations; whereas in the past the vast majority have been weeded out after two years by the tenth-year examination. Now the policy is to try to let everyone stay to the end of the fourth year. This will expand secondary education enormously if it is achieved.

3. Far from taking away jobs from any qualified African teachers, this program is making possible the more rapid Africanization or localization of the educational system at the administrative level as independence has approached or been achieved. Upon the arrival of TEA teachers in the schools African teachers could be moved into responsible administrative posts to replace British personnel without reducing the number of qualified teachers in the schools.

I was assured that this program was not only aiding Africanization of administrative posts in education but in other public service positions as well. There are two priorities for a transitional nation that becomes independent and seeks to rule itself with justice and freedom: first, it must have a qualified set of public administrators; and second, it must have a good educational system. TEA is serving both these ends by making it possible for some of the most highly educated Africans, namely, the teachers, to move into positions of public administration and by helping to strengthen and expand the educational system itself. I am convinced that this is one of the most important aspects of the whole project.

4. TEA is helping to make possible not only the expansion of secondary education but the expansion of teacher training as well. The job of the TEA teachers, in the long run, is not to run the schools or even to teach in the schools of East Africa, but to make it possible for the East African countries to train their own teachers and to run their own schools. Wherever we went the point was made that there are not enough graduates of secondary schools to man all the positions the new countries need. It is sad but true that many of those who successfully complete secondary school will not go into teaching so long as there are more remunerative and powerful posts to be had. It is thus argued that more young people will be attracted into teaching only when the production of the secondary schools is so great that key governmental, administrative, professional, and commercial positions can first be reasonably well filled. Unfortunately, we know too well that this situation is not confined to East Africa and that teacher training sometimes comes off second best in the United States as well as almost everywhere else.

The way to overcome this situation, therefore, is to send as many good students as possible through secondary school so that responsible public positions of many kinds can be adequately manned as soon as possible. As these jobs begin to be filled more secondary school leavers will turn to teacher training. It will take several years and a continuing supply of expatriate teachers to enable the secondary schools to expand and thus provide enough secondary school leavers who can be trained as teachers to enable the new countries to man their secondary schools themselves. Through this essential process of development TEA contributes to teacher training. I am also glad to say that we have been able to contribute even more directly to the training of teachers, for some of the TEA teachers are teaching academic subjects in teacher training colleges as well as in secondary schools.

5. The effect of American teachers upon the curriculum and the

methods of teaching in the schools will be greater and will come sooner, I think, than we had expected. This change is welcomed by some and, naturally, looked upon with skepticism by others. In 1961 a school staff may have consisted of six British members, six Africans, and one or two Americans. The prospect was that one or two of the British were uncertain about their future plans and might not come back from their home leaves; one or two of the Africans were hoping to move out and up into other jobs, and one or two new Americans were on their way in. As early as the end of 1962 some of the schools had staffs in which a major voice was that of TEA teachers. Some TEA teachers were the senior masters in their fields—simply because of their qualifications. In other schools, because of the turnover of staff, it is entirely possible that TEA teachers will soon become the senior masters in length of service.

In a time of great uncertainty and change TEA is injecting a useful element of stability into the system. As the American teachers become accepted as regular members of staff and knowledgeable about the curriculum and methods of teaching, some of them are being asked not only to draw up new syllabuses and new materials but to revise and improve the old in collaboration with their British and African colleagues. This is the way genuine change comes about in an educational system—by professionals who are working within the system and know what they are doing—not by the importation of foreign packages of educational materials, even if they are gift packages.

6. Finally, the last word is something difficult to define but important. The testimony on many sides seems to be that one of the most significant contributions of the American teachers is the infusion of a new spirit into the schools. Their enthusiasm, energy, conscientiousness, hopefulness, hard work, and optimism are bringing a new sense of life and vitality to schools that have been dispirited and discouraged by an uncertain future, by a chronic shortage of staff, by underpay, and by overwork. Because of the uncertain political future for some British expatriate teachers and because of the hope of some of the African staff to move elsewhere, there has been in more than

a few schools an attitude of simply marking time. There is also the hold-over of a resigned civil servant spirit on the part of many staff members who had originally come out simply to do a job, to go where they were told to go, and to do what they were told to do, but who put no particular zeal or zest into their performance, and are simply waiting to be able to claim their compensation before they go home.

I think that the students sense a different kind of attitude on the part of the American teachers. This testimony has come from headmasters as well as from other staff members. Very often it was easy to see a sign of new hope in the schools, often it centered around TEA teachers, British as well as American, working together with their African colleagues. I believe that a new sense of enthusiasm, zest, and dedication to the job of teaching is making itself felt. I believe that the TEA is having a significant role in igniting this spirit, and in the long run it may be the most important contribution that can be made to nations that would rule themselves by educating themselves.

PEACE CORPS VOLUNTEERS

Much of what I have just said about the Teachers for East Africa project could also be said of hundreds of Peace Corps volunteers who are teaching in the elementary and secondary schools of many countries of the world. I visited briefly some fifty Peace Corps teachers in West Africa in January 1962, and I was director of studies for the Nigeria VI training program at Teachers College in the fall of 1962. Even though I cannot speak with as much assurance about the Peace Corps, for I have not had as much direct or extended personal contact with it as with TEA, I believe strongly in the value of both programs. TEA, which has had relatively little written about it in the public or professional press,[2] was soon overshadowed in numbers and in public attention by the Peace Corps with its captivating program, its energetic leadership, its commendations from the White House,

---

[2] See Gertrude Samuels, "To Meet Africa's Great Need—Education," *The New York Times Magazine*, August 20, 1961; and "In Answer to Africa's Need for Teachers," *The New York Times Magazine*, March 18, 1962.

its attractiveness to the college campuses, its enthusiastic and dedicated staff, and its public relations experts.

The Peace Corps has rapidly become one of the exciting new ventures in American international life and education—and deserves to be recognized as such. It has its own publications and its own publicity organs, and it has had a great deal written about it in the popular press. It undoubtedly will also inspire a considerable amount of serious study and research which will result in an increased flow of scholarly publications in the future. Eventually it ought to be possible for some exceedingly interesting comparisons to be made between the various Peace Corps projects and those of TEA.

I believe that a principal difference between the Peace Corps' outlook on overseas teachers and TEA's is that the latter was conceived and carried out largely by professionals in the field of education. This may not necessarily make it better or worse, but it does mean that the entire framework of thought and planning in TEA was aimed at discovering the best way to select and train qualified American professionals to work within an existing but different educational system and on a level of parity with the other trained professionals already in the system. The Peace Corps, on the other hand, has been largely aimed at providing opportunity for Americans to volunteer their services to help and to understand other peoples on a non-career, temporary, emergency basis. The Peace Corps' approach to teaching has been to send overseas able and versatile young American volunteers most of whom had given no thought to teaching until the Peace Corps offered them a chance to go overseas to do it. On the other hand, most of those in TEA are already qualified teachers who wish to carry on their profession in Africa for a time as a means of providing international educational service to another country.

The Peace Corps' mandate from Congress has three purposes which serve to highlight these differences. Its first purpose is to provide "skills" to other countries. This can, of course, be interpreted to include teaching skills, but the original intention was far broader than teaching. Indeed, in the early days of the Peace Corps, the non-teaching skills of working with the hands and doing manual labor in the villages of the world seemed to dominate the publicity about the Peace Corps. Furthermore, "skills" are interpreted to mean the skills of "middle-level manpower" in contrast to the high-level professional knowledge and technical competence which presumably are the provinces of the technical assistance programs of AID. In a real sense, then, the Peace Corps does not look upon teaching as a profession but as a skill and as a "middle-level" skill at that. The trouble is that secondary school teaching in many of the underdeveloped countries of the world is esteemed more highly than it is in the United States; it is considered to be a relatively *high*-level profession requiring a university degree and at least a year of professional training on top of the degree. Few professions require as much education and professional training, and only a small number of individuals in the emerging countries have so far achieved the status of university graduate as compared with those in the United States.

Still more important, the Peace Corps looks upon the volunteer service as a non-career endeavor by means of which Americans can serve their own country by several months of voluntary work and sacrifice in another country. The second and third purposes of the Peace Corps are to increase understanding of Americans by other peoples and to increase understanding of other peoples by Americans. These are essentially motives that underlie the cultural exchange programs discussed in the first chapter of this book. But something new has been added to international understanding by the Peace Corps: an emphasis upon living and working as the people of the host countries do rather than living as American tourists or officials do or even as American professors and students do. This has played an extremely important and effective part in the Peace Corps' goal to change the image of Americans overseas. But it has sometimes not been applicable to secondary school teachers; for African teachers and British expatriate teachers in Africa often do not relish behavior by Americans which they view as undercutting their status as highly trained professionals and thereby reducing their effectiveness in their schools and in their communities.

The stream of announcements and statements designed to promote recruitment in the Peace Corps has constantly stressed the importance of community service and international understanding and has underplayed the importance of professional competence. This emphasis has often dominated the discussion about teaching by Peace Corps officials.

Many of the early publications of the Peace Corps exhibited something of an offhand spirit when referring to teaching as the job of prospective volunteers. The tone often ran something like this: "Join the Peace Corps to serve the common people of other lands and thus aid understanding between them and the United States. Live and work with them on their terms. If they want teachers, you can be a teacher. You really do not need prior professional education; you can get all you need in a few weeks of Peace Corps training. Much more important than professional training are your personal qualities, your motivation, and your skills in interpersonal relations."

A brochure sent out by the Peace Corps in March 1963 addressed to liberal arts students entitled *College Education—PLUS* put it this way:

> The Peace Corps, it is true, does need specialists—doctors, nurses, engineers, carpenters, etc. But Americans with no developed "skill" as we commonly use the term, but who have leadership abilities, initiative, and resourcefulness can serve effectively in many areas.

THE PLUS FACTORS

What are some of the plus factors of a liberal arts education that will help qualify you for a Peace Corps assignment?

Participation in youth and recreation activities, a farm background, leadership roles in social, civic or church groups, basic do-it-yourself skills in carpentry, mechanics, gardening, handcraft, home economics, first aid, hygiene, experience in organizing committees, electing officers, organizing a library group or a PTA. And most importantly, the self-confidence that comes from your knowledge that you can get a job done, or that you can find a source of information that tells you how to do it.

Topping the plus factors, of course, are personal characteristics of ingenuity, initiative, versatility—and the sincere desire to serve people in need.

TEACHING IN THE PEACE CORPS

Peace Corps Volunteer teachers differ from other American educators working abroad through exchange, private or government programs. Generally, teachers in these other programs function as specialists or advisors to the host country governments, or as technical assistants. But Peace Corps Volunteers work side-by-side with nationals. Each Volunteer works under the direction of the principal or headmaster of the school in which he teaches.

Prior teaching experience is not required for most assignments. College graduates with liberal arts training fill most of the requests.

Since all Volunteers participate actively in the community life of the city or village of their assignment, avocational interests and experience are important. Many Volunteer teachers, for example, coach sports, conduct youth recreation programs, teach adult education courses, and help organize community groups to meet local problems. It is in this area of broader involvement that the liberal arts graduate assigned to teach can effectively apply the plus values of practical experience to his specific task of teaching.

It is small wonder that liberal arts graduates may be tempted to take lightly the teaching part of the job and to assume that other values than day-by-day classroom teaching are the things that really matter in Peace Corps service. Their negative attitudes about the need for professional training for teaching, often encouraged in their liberal arts colleges, seem to be confirmed by the Peace Corps appeal. I found this attitude strong among the first volunteers to be sent to teach in West Africa. Some I spoke to in the early weeks of their assignments were supremely confident that they would be able to do a good job, that they did not particularly need any direct training for teaching other than subject matter. This outlook was strongly encouraged by the Peace Corps representative in some countries. Few of the original volunteers had had any intention of teaching before they joined the Peace Corps, some took a teaching assignment in the particular country concerned as a second or third choice, few had any intention of teaching when they returned to the United States, others were incensed at the idea that they might be observed in their classrooms as a means of judging their effectiveness as teachers. Still others felt that since they were going to be there only two years, it would be a waste of time to give them much training.

This attitude has continued among some volunteers and appears in the evaluation being made in one country by a study of teaching effectiveness which was based wholly on interviews with the volunteers and did not include the expert judgments of the responsible administrative officers in the schools or in the ministry of education, the volunteer's colleagues, the responses of students or their achievements on the examinations, or firsthand observation of teaching performance.

Interestingly enough, many volunteers, once on the job, have testified that they wished they had had more direct training for teaching before they arrived at their school. Careful studies of teaching effectiveness will, I hope, be made for all Peace Corps teaching projects. I am convinced, however, that the testimony revealed in the following letter from a woman volunteer in West Africa must not be ignored:

My posting is the . . . Teacher Training College, where I teach English 28 periods a week. My classes are year 1A, 2, and 4. Teaching is at once challenging, frustrating and exciting. I find myself rushing from my house to the college early every morning in hopes that I will succeed at the day's classes. Sometimes I fall flat on my face and sometimes, but only occasionally, I feel as if I get across to the boys. (We have only 9 girls at the school.) I enjoy years 1 and 2 very much, for I always feel that win, draw or lose we work as a team. But the year 4's are somewhat of a burden. They are all either the same age as I, or older. Many of them are married and have children. Also they have been teaching before they came to the college to work on their grade two certificates. These facts do not make my teaching them very easy. They are very much more apt to challenge than learn. But I am determined to reach them somehow. It is the "somehow" that is my main problem. P.C. training fitted me very well for the climate, politics, living, and culture of . . . but I am sadly lacking in teaching method and technique. In short I was prepared for everything except my job. This is paradoxical since I have to observe the practice teaching and write comments both for the boys and the school. I rack my brain constantly trying to recall things from the training dealing with method and teaching English as a foreign language but find that there is not much to recall. I also spend a good deal of time just learning

English grammar, which I have not had since I was a sophomore in high school. Shakespeare, Chaucer, and American Literature have minor importance at this level. I marvel that the Peace Corps feels it can send inexperienced people like myself out here without giving them any more training in education—of a practical nature—than they do. . . . Perhaps experience is the best teacher, but learning at the expense of these boys is disturbing to say the least.

Aside from the teaching everything is fine.

In fact I have the feeling that many of the early Peace Corps officials were surprised to find that despite their appeal to American youth for unselfish service to our country what so many of the other countries wanted was service to their countries, not of unskilled labor or semiskilled workers but of qualified teachers. In April of 1963 more than half (52 per cent) of the 5,000 Peace Corps volunteers were in teaching projects; nearly a third (31 per cent) in secondary school teaching alone. It has apparently been difficult for some Peace Corps officials to readjust their preconceptions to the fact that professional qualifications for teaching overseas are not only deemed necessary in some underdeveloped countries but they cannot be acquired overnight.

Some of the early training programs for Peace Corps volunteers were not adequately designed and were too short for those who were to be secondary school teachers in highly structured school systems. The contract requirements of the Peace Corps give heavy weight to area studies, American studies, understanding of communism, physical and health education, and language study, but relatively little attention to "technical studies"; i.e., acquiring competence in the particular job to be done. This outlook seemed to be coupled with the belief on the part of some Peace Corps officials that any liberal arts college graduate could teach almost anything overseas, even if he had no professional training.

In all fairness it must be said, too, that the education component where it did appear in the earlier training programs was likely to be rated as the poorest part of the program by the trainees themselves. We still have a long way to go in overcoming the inherited academic prejudice against professional education; and professional educators should do much more than lament the fact that their liberal arts colleagues instill such attitudes in their students.

The American graduate schools of education have not been nearly as alert to the possibilities in Peace Corps training as they should be. Some have held back because of suspicion or hostility toward what they believed to be the Peace Corps denigration of professional training and professional qualifications for teachers. Others have held back from sheer indifference to their international responsibilities. Still others have simply been preoccupied with their "regular" programs. They have not been nearly so eager to take part in the training programs as the area study and language specialists have been. Or, when the professional educators *have* taken part, the results of the "education" units have too often been of such low quality in the view of the volunteers that their preconceptions have been confirmed and even heightened. This in turn has served to strengthen the attitude of some Peace Corps officials and training directors that the "education" units are not necessary or not desirable.

This relationship between schools of education and overseas training programs like the Peace Corps should be radically improved. In earlier chapters of this book I have urged the schools of education to improve their role in international studies, in advancement of knowledge about world affairs, in academic interchanges, in educational assistance programs sponsored by AID, and in research in educational development. I believe that they must also become concerned with improving their role in the training of teachers for overseas educational service. Just as all AID "technicians" must become "educators," so all Peace Corps volunteers are in a sense "teachers." No matter what the volunteer does, he is engaged in informal teaching even if not formal teaching. He is also a representative of American education as much as he is a representative of American life and culture. Every volunteer should study about American education just as he studies about American life and institutions in general. Every volunteer should know about the educational systems and aspirations of the people of the host country just as he should know about the host country's politics, economics, and foreign relations.

The estrangement of the Peace Corps and university schools of education has been by no means a one-sided affair. *Rapprochement* requires the strenuous efforts of both. I see some heartening signs of this. Educators should realize that the Peace Corps is trying to deal with a great range and variety of training programs and that all countries do not require exactly the same kind of professional training for teachers, but the Peace Corps must realize too that the countries differ and that the training of teachers for those countries which require high qualifications for teachers in a structured educational system may be different from the training required for a country where the level of education is lower and the educational structure is less developed.

The original Peace Corps attitude toward professional education coupled with an impatience toward slow-moving university methods and academic customs led to some clashes between Peace Corps and university officials in the early days. Indeed a few universities refused to go through the hair-raising process of conducting a Peace Corps training program a second time. My own institution was one of these. But, after further discussion and a good deal of second thinking on both sides, I am glad to say that Teachers College is again working closely and, I may add, harmoniously with the Peace Corps Training Division. I am especially pleased that our convictions were honored by the Peace Corps in the training programs we have recently conducted for secondary school teaching in Nigeria. These have included lengthening the training program for untrained teachers, providing larger and improved ingredients of professional education and practice teaching, and treating the untrained liberal arts graduate differently from the professionally trained teacher so that a stronger professional commitment could be built.

Let me quote what I said to the trainees in the introductory statement of our syllabus for Nigeria VI:

This training program is designed to prepare you, within a short period of time, to do the best possible job of teaching in the secondary schools of Nigeria.

It is, admittedly, not a full fledged course of professional education. It does not meet the usual standards expected of fully qualified secondary school teachers, either in Nigeria or in the United States. It is frankly an emergency training program to enable you speedily to help meet the critical need for teachers in Nigeria.

The need is great, the request is urgent, and the Peace Corps has undertaken to respond to the request quickly. Teachers College is undertaking to respond with the same sense of speed and urgency but at the same time to design a program that will be professionally acceptable even though it has had to be squeezed into a condensed and concentrated form.

In line with British educational traditions the requirements for fully qualified secondary school teachers in Nigeria have consisted of at least a year of professional training in addition to a university degree. . . .

In view of the prevalence of such standards as these a training program for Peace Corps Trainees which is shorter than customary in Nigeria but which will be acceptable to the expectations of Nigerian educational officials must be experimental. It must strike a balance between the exigencies of a speeded-up program to meet the emergency and a standard of academic and professional excellence that will maintain quality. If possible, it should also help you to give assistance in the expansion of educational opportunity and in the development of an education appropriate to the aspirations of a new nation.

You are American Peace Corps Trainees who will be assigned to teach for a relatively short period of time in a country that is probably unfamiliar to most of you. You will be Americans in schools where the staffs will consist of a mixture of Nigerian, British, and possibly other European or Asian nationalities.

As Peace Corps members you will be marked with high visibility among other Americans in and out of schools. As Volunteers you will be joining staffs which have traditionally consisted of a corps of career teachers who have often been teaching for years and who expected to continue to do so, until recently.

As expatriates you will be guests of a country where the position of secondary school teachers has a high status and is open to only a relatively few well educated Nigerians.

EDUCATION STUDIES

The Education Studies will aid you in becoming familiar with the job of teaching you will be expected to do. This is a peculiarly sensitive and difficult task. The educational system is different in many respects from ours. The background, language, and aspirations of the students are likely to be unfamiliar, and the conduct and customs of the schools are quite different from those of American schools.

On top of these differences most of you will have had no training or experience in teaching in the United States. The Education Studies will try to induct you into the strange and wonderful world of teaching with its peculiar combination of frustrations and fascinations. Teachers and lecturers from Nigeria and experienced American teachers and administrators will add their experience to that of the subject-matter specialists who will put you through your professional paces. The success of the entire undertaking depends in the final analysis upon how well you perform as a teacher. . . .

We know that you are anxious to be on your way to Nigeria. We know that the training program will seem long to many of you—possibly far too long to some. But, becoming an international teacher is a most complicated, tricky, and sensitive business. Teaching in another culture is not simply an occasion for a slow motion travel tour nor something that can be improvised on the spot. It takes the most careful kind of study, reflection, discussion, and special preparation. We expect you to do a great deal of all of these. In fact the whole training program is considered by the Peace Corps to be a major part of the selection process for overseas service as Volunteers.

The United States is relatively new in the large-scale enterprise of selecting, training, and sending teachers overseas. We must learn rapidly and we must learn well. We shall undoubtedly make some mistakes. You not only have the enviable chance to take part in the shaping of a remarkable new development in international education, but because you have joined up fairly early in the process, you can be very useful in improving the programs for those who will follow. We welcome your suggestions and criticisms.

By the spring of 1963 more than fifty universities had been involved and more than six hundred social scientists had taken part in Peace Corps training programs. And the end was nowhere in sight. There is no doubt that these represented more extensive and more intensive training for non-career overseas service than has ever before been provided with the possible exception of military training for inductees. No doubt these training programs will have important effects upon career-training programs as well as upon the area studies programs of colleges and universities.

The graduate schools of education and the Peace Corps may be over the hump on the problem of professional training for Peace

Corps teachers. Numerous statements by Joseph Kauffman, director of the training division, and by Robert W. Iversen, deputy director, as well as the effective cooperation of such training officers as Robert Binswanger are testimonies to improved relationships between universities and the Peace Corps. If the Peace Corps could accelerate the direction thus begun, I am convinced that universities would enter even more enthusiastically into the training process than they have done so far.

In the first two years the Peace Corps was understandably anxious to respond quickly to urgent requests for large numbers of volunteers to show that America cared. This led it to be impatient with the equally understandable desire of universities to be sure that the trainees sent out under their auspices would be well prepared for the professional tasks they were being asked to perform. Universities uniformly wanted a longer time to get ready and a longer period for the programs themselves. For example, I think it would be much better if the volunteers who were to be teachers were asked to serve for two academic school years *after* training rather than to deduct the training period from their two years of service. The present policy keeps up the pressure for a shorter training period and may tend to pull volunteers out of their schools in the middle of a term, leaving the students shortchanged—or if the term of service is extended to the end of the school term, the volunteer feels that the rules have been changed and *he* is being imposed upon. It may be one thing to bring a volunteer home almost any time from an unstructured community development project; it is another thing to pull a teacher out of a school term.

The Peace Corps seems to be settling for twelve to fifteen weeks of training for teachers. I can live with this policy if the trainees are well selected. I still believe that the training institutions should have more to do with selection. A great deal can be done in an intensive course with a well motivated group in three months (virtually a full academic semester). I cannot agree that we can do as well in twelve weeks of intensive activity what we can do in an academic year that would provide much more time for systematic thought and reading in international, area, and American studies as well as for discipline in the theory and practice of professional education.

As a temporary measure to meet the emergency need for teachers around the world I believe that the training we are now giving to well selected trainees will enable them to do a good job of teaching and in some cases an excellent job. But the time has come to regularize training, give up the emergency stance, and look upon the provision of teachers for developing countries as a process that must be planned as a whole, beginning with selection, training, and assignment to posts, and extending to supervision, in-service training on the job, and return to the United States.

This requires the closest kind of continuing cooperation between the government concerned, the Peace Corps, and the university professional school of education. None of these three can go it alone. Arrangements should be made for longer term contracts so that such cooperation can be achieved. Many host governments, I am sure, would now say to the Peace Corps: "Please be sure that the volunteer teachers really have the skill and qualifications necessary for good teaching. Good will is not enough. It is better to go a little slower in order to be sure of solid preparation. You have proved that you can respond quickly and effectively; please now prove that you can continue to respond well with high quality."

I am convinced that a non-career voluntary service is the only way we can supply enough teachers to meet the emergency needs of many countries for the next few years. Provision of fully qualified teachers, trained in the usual way and meeting the usual requirements for qualified teachers, will not be enough to do the job. I am therefore equally interested in trying to design training programs for non-careerists as well as for careerists. I am equally interested in TEA and in the Peace Corps. But, by the same token, I believe the Peace Corps should not play down the dimensions of the teaching job itself, as Peace Corps publicity tends to do; it should be played up. The Peace Corps has proved the devotion of American youth to service; now let us prove their devotion to the most important job in emerging countries. Even if we cannot insist upon a long-term career commitment to teaching, let us try to get a real commitment to teaching for the period of service; and let us make the period of teaching a full two academic years. Many volunteers, I am afraid, do not particularly want to teach, but they *do* really want to serve. Unless they can genuinely accept teaching as the *best* way to serve, they should not go as teachers.

I still hope that the Peace Corps will modify its stand on such points as the following: the small role it allows to training institutions in the selection of trainees; the overweening emphasis on psychiatric analysis during the training programs; the intense anxieties raised by overemphasizing the fact that the training period is basically a part of final selection; too great emphasis upon building "quotas" in record time for particular countries, which leads to a reluctance to make long-term and integrated plans for selection and training and assignment; the apparent prejudice against in-country training for teachers and the insistence that on-the-ground orientation must be short because the volunteer is anxious to get on with the job; and insufficient emphasis upon in-service training and professional support while on the job.

I have no better way of summing up what I have said than to quote a most discerning letter that has been written by a Harvard man who went through our training program for Nigeria VI in the fall of 1962. I believe it states well the case for attracting to the Peace Corps college graduates who not only want to serve but who want to serve by doing a responsible job of teaching:

I found training generally excellent. My principal criticism is that we encountered too much theory, by proportion. Much of the credit must go to the training staff at Columbia Teachers College (credit both for the overall quality of the program and for the preponderance of theory). I found training to be a reasonable intellectual challenge and a great psychological one. The physical activities we were expected to engage in were rather less than I expected—it seems as though the Peace Corps is satisfied to send semi-fit people to teach. We concentrated on developing teaching skills, not on 10 mile hikes or similar endurance trials. As only two or three of the group had any teaching experience, this was obviously necessary. Having taught for six weeks, I am now very appreciative of that teaching preparation, though, like others at the time, I felt it less worthwhile than the "solid" subjects we did: African history and politics, international affairs, and American Government. Our program lasted twelve weeks and we were accorded the dividend of nine credits from CTC. It seemed to me to be genuine academic experience, valuable apart from the utilitarian aspect of preparation for overseas—though I must interject that other PC training programs I've heard described were not nearly as successful from the academic standpoint. It may be that our program was a great improvement over earlier programs, but I can't say. . . .

My school is . . . beginning its third year, has 120 boys (two streams in class I) and six tutors. The principal and I are the only graduates on the staff and I'm the only expatriate (read European or white man) at school or in the town. My subjects, at present, are: English (I A & B), French (I A & B), chemistry (III), Oral English (II), and History (II). I began doing Latin instead of chemistry, but we've had three changes of schedule already and perhaps more on the way. Incidentally, I also taught algebra for a week. English is chiefly composition since literature is a separate subject. . . . I also coach track, tennis, and ping pong (the latter has considerable standing over here). Next term, with the help of equipment provided by the Peace Corps, I intend to introduce softball, basketball, and volleyball. I teach 24 forty minute periods a week, and don't have any additional supervisory duties since I'm the only staff member not living on the compound. Like most schools here, mine is residential. . . .

Subject matter is presented at the same level as in English secondary schools which means that it demands enough of the teacher to keep him interested, even at the lower forms. I had apprehensions on this score that happily were not realized. There is no discipline problem for me, though many other PCVs in Nigeria complain of one. . . . I can say without any qualifications that I'm satisfied with my job and what it requires of me. . . .

I personally feel that the value of my experience is inestimable, and I have no reservations about recommending the Peace Corps (or any of several other programs) to anyone who can postpone law or medical school long enough to undertake it. It is quite important, though, that anyone who intends to do this kind of thing realizes that he must derive the most of his satisfaction out of the job he fills. That is, your everyday occupation while you're serving abroad will absorb most of your time and energy—if you can't also give it your full interest I think you're likely to be dissatisfied. Two years spent doing something you aren't genuinely interested in would be trying under any circumstances. If you volunteer to be a teacher, I think you'd better be prepared to treat the work very seriously.[3]

If an increasing number of American graduates can be encouraged to volunteer for *teaching in the Peace Corps* in the spirit expressed in the foregoing letter, I have great confidence that a genuine service can be performed in the development of nations. There is room for both the career international teacher represented by TEA and the non-career volunteer for teaching represented by the Peace Corps. The differences, however, should be clearly understood and proper training for each provided. In both cases preparation will be improved if colleges, universities, and graduate schools of education take the steps to improve their international studies and their preparation for educational development as proposed in the first two chapters of this book. The special training programs would then not be obliged to fill so many academic gaps by intensive measures and could give greater attention to relating academic preparation to professional tasks.

The decision seems to have been made in Washington that AID will provide high-level professional advice and consultants in educational development to other nations through its programs of technical assistance and that the Peace Corps will provide middle-level skills at the operational level of "doing." And teaching in the schools seems to fall in Peace Corps hands as a "middle-level operational skill."

This division of labor does not give careful enough attention to teaching as a professional task in overseas secondary schools. The proper division of labor in development education would be between the career motive and the non-career motive. This would mean that AID as the major American agency for educational development within technical assistance would enlist university aid in supplying educators at both the consultative and operational level wherever career teachers as well as career consultants are required. This

---

[3] A letter to Harvard University from a 1961 graduate, Roger M. Leed, who was a member of the Nigeria VI Peace Corps training program at Teachers College and is teaching in Nigeria.

"career" motive may include an overseas career in education as such or it may apply to career educators who wish to devote a share of their professional life to overseas consultation, administration, or teaching. It could include elementary and secondary school teaching as well as university teaching. In either case the education, training, and commitment should live up to the highest qualifications required by professional careerists anywhere in the world. These require more than "middle-level skills." As I have said earlier, educational development could thus draw upon both the technical assistance approach and the direct service approach.

Overseas, the educational assistance activities of AID and the operations of the Peace Corps could well be coordinated for the benefit of all concerned. In Afghanistan, for example, the Teachers College team has been engaging in the teaching of English in secondary schools and developing appropriate instructional materials for the teaching of English to Afghans. As the Peace Corps takes up the English teaching functions in the schools it is essential that the accumulated knowledge, experience, and competence of the Teachers College professional team be drawn upon for the benefit of the inexperienced Peace Corps teachers. A report by Professor John Polley, head of the Teachers College team in Afghanistan, describes a desirable relationship this way:

For some months Americans in Afghanistan have looked forward to the arrival of members of the Peace Corps. The Peace Corps has won an enviable reputation in other parts of the world as the result of successful efforts. The TCCU Team is particularly concerned with fitting Peace Corps personnel into what, we believe, is a carefully worked out plan for teaching English in Afghanistan. The arrival of the first five Peace Corps English teachers and their careful induction into teaching English in Afghanistan under the guidance of experienced teachers who know both classroom problems and the technical field of teaching English as a second language is being successfully carried on. Members of the TCCU Team have been anxious to help wherever they can. The members of the Peace Corps have been anxious to have this help. The Ministry of Education has thoughtfully refrained from putting these teachers into immediate service in the classroom and has allowed an ample period of orientation. The Peace Corps English teachers will be thoroughly familiar with the material which they use in the classroom and with the problems and procedures which preceding teachers have encountered and evolved.

On their arrival in Kabul the Peace Corps teachers were given a two week orientation by members of the English Language staff of the TCCU Team. Following this they were given practice under supervision in classroom teaching. During this same time they worked on the preparation of a textbook series for the teaching of English as a second language in Afghanistan. All of this induction process contributed to an understanding of how English is taught and to the problems in teaching it which are peculiar to Afghanistan.

If encouraged by the host countries and the respective American agencies, this pattern of operation could set a most desirable precedent of inter-agency cooperation whereby the experienced AID university team of career educational advisers provides professional guidance for the inexperienced and non-career Peace Corps teachers. University contract teams in the field may be a better means of overcoming inter-agency rivalries than the tables of organization or reorganization plans designed in Washington.

Thus, I would strongly urge that AID *improve* its operational activities in providing direct educational service, as is done in the TEA, not give up such activities. A coordinated program of educational development planning and regular teaching service can usefully enhance the quality of both. In some circumstances such coordination may be accomplished more effectively if both types of activity are under the auspices of a single university; similarly, a university itself may be the best means of coordinating activities supported by both AID and Peace Corps. In any case the *professional* role of the university should be paramount in working with and for the host country.

For its part, the Peace Corps can be immensely valuable in providing non-career volunteers who wish to take seriously the professional task of teaching overseas to meet present emergencies and who are willing to spend the time to equip themselves for the task by three to four months of training and at least two years of service. In the overseas setting their service should be closely coordinated with the host government's own planning as well as with the technical assistance planning undertaken with AID and other agencies. If the Peace Corps would also permit volunteers to remain on for a period of time beyond the two years (a period which brings them to a peak of teaching usefulness), it would serve the developing nations well indeed.

And if many volunteers could be drawn into teaching or into further international studies in the United States upon their return,[4] the cause of international development would be doubly served as the volunteers direct their energies at helping to develop *American* education and thereby contribute to a developing American nationhood. Peace Corps training programs for teachers should thus redouble their efforts to instill a positive professional motivation among the trainees as well as develop the greatest possible professional competence in a short time. Peace Corps training and overseas service in teaching could then be looked upon not simply as an interim way to render overseas service in general, but could be looked upon as the *first steps* in building a professional career in education—which, as I shall try to indicate in the final chapter, is an essential requirement for *any* nation that would be both modern and free. If this should happen, if the flow of TEA and Peace Corps teachers into American education can be stimulated upon their return, America's troika of international studies, educational development, and overseas teaching will have been truly harnessed to a kind of international development that serves the aider as well as it serves the aided.

[4] Hopefully, the new programs of fellowships instituted by individual colleges and universities will serve this cause. Of especial interest is the announcement that seventy-five graduate fellowships have been made available with Ford money for those who have served more than a year in overseas service in an underdeveloped country. The priority fields of study are education, economics, public administration, community development, public health, and English as a second language. Participating institutions are Columbia, Harvard, Cornell, Stanford, Chicago, UCLA, North Carolina, and Penn State. The program is called Study Fellowships for International Development with headquarters at Pennsylvania State University.

To assist returnees to obtain suitable positions in education, government and public service, and business, the American Council on Education established in the summer of 1963 the Peace Corps Volunteer Career Information Service, supported for the first year by the Carnegie Corporation and located at 700 Jackson Place, Washington, D.C.

❦ 4 ❦

Self-education:
The Goal of Development

In the foregoing chapters I have tried to describe the three major drives of American education in the international arena and to state some propositions concerning what American education and especially what American teacher education should be doing in the future. In general I have confronted the problem of international education from the point of view of America and of American education. In this final chapter I should like to view the problems of education as they must be faced by the developing nations themselves. In doing so I would like to suggest, on one hand, how the accumulating knowledge of the social sciences and international studies may have a bearing on their solution and, on the other hand, how educational advisers, development educators, and expatriate teachers may be of assistance in the process of educational development. I assume throughout, however, that the new nations, if they are to be genuinely free, must determine their own educational goals and develop their own educational systems. Free peoples must educate themselves.

I have no intention of prescribing the goals, content, or methods of education for other countries. But I would like to mention some problems which I believe should be faced candidly and courageously by those who plan and design their own educational systems for themselves and by those who undertake to give assistance to the educational planners of other countries. It may be that America's troika in international education may be more useful in the development of nations than has so far been contemplated, but, I repeat, all educational assistance should lead to self-education. Otherwise, it is not educational assistance.

National planning for education will take form within settings often marked by wide divergences of opinion and interest. Each country striving for modernization already has a more or less well developed educational system usually modeled in some part upon or imported from Western European sources, principally British or French. Each new nation has its own aspirations for a national style built upon its sense of traditional values, its sense of need for modernization of its economy, polity, and society, the extent of its desire to be independent of former colonial rule and to maintain an open, free society of its own, its determination to become a unified nation-state, the varying ambitions of its political leaders for their nation or for themselves, and its image of the international role it wishes to play in the comity of nations.

Some of the modernizing countries are making an inventory of their resources, are setting up three- or five-year plans for development as well as long-range plans, and are estimating what they can do and should do by their own efforts, and what they need and can expect from outside help. Some countries have asked for surveys and advice from the World Bank, or the United Nations, or UNESCO, or they have set up some other expert special advisory commission to assist with their planning. Needless to say, the advice from different sources is sometimes contradictory, or sometimes is made in ignorance of or indifference to the advice from other quarters. Plans for education sometimes suffer from these differences of opinion or somehow are not always related to total development plans.

On the positive side, however, many recent and important conferences have been held and assessments of the needs and goals for education have been made by the developing countries.[1] I cannot, of

---

[1] See, for example, *Investment in Education.* The Report of the [Ashby] Commission on Pre-School Certificate and Higher Education in Nigeria (Lagos, Nigeria: Federal Ministry of Education, 1960); UNESCO, Conference of African States on the Development of Education in Africa, *Final Report* (Addis

course, deal with such plans and proposals here, but several things are clear: The underdeveloped countries are determined to expand their educational systems as rapidly as possible. They speak of universal primary education by 1970 or 1980 and substantial increases in secondary and higher education. They are hoping to increase the amount of money they spend on education until they assign as much as 4 or 5 per cent of their gross national products to education. They state that education should be planned integrally with the other plans for economic and national development. They are particularly concerned that education contribute to economic growth by new stress upon science and technical education, rural and agricultural education, adult education, or education for such disadvantaged groups as girls and tribal peoples. They also express interest in conducting educational research and exploring the use of new technologies in educational method, such as film strips, motion pictures, radio, television, and programed instruction as means of speeding up instruction at a lower cost.

The African states are particularly concerned to expand facilities for secondary education, for higher education, and for teacher training. They speak of the need for reform of the curriculum "to make it

---

Ababa, May 15–25, 1961); UNESCO, Meeting of Ministers of Education of African Countries Participating in the Implementation of the Addis Ababa Plan, Final Report, (Paris, March 26–30, 1962); UNESCO, Conclusions and Recommendations of the Conference on the Development of Higher Education in Africa, The Development of Higher Education in Africa, (Tananarive, September 3–12, 1962); a short summary of the Tananarive Report has been prepared by Sir Alexander Carr-Saunders under the title of Staffing African Universities (Washington, D.C.; American Council on Education, 1963); the May 1962 issue of UNESCO Chronicle contains summaries of the Santiago Declaration of the Latin American countries, the Tokyo and Karachi meetings of Asian states, and the Addis Ababa and Paris meetings of African countries; Organization of American States, Alliance for Progress, Official Documents emanating from the Special Meeting of the Inter-American Economic and Social Council at the Ministerial Level, held at Punta del Este, Uruguay, August 5–17, 1961 (Washington, D.C.: Pan-American Union, 1961); Organization of American States, Latin American Higher Education and Inter-American Cooperation (Washington, D.C.: Pan-American Union, 1961); and Council on Higher Education in the American Republics and Institute of International Education, Educational Needs in Latin America (Princeton, N.J.: Princeton University Press, December 1961).

more responsive to the needs of a changing society and more appropriate to the needs for structural changes in the existing economies."[2] This suggests that the curriculum should pay more attention to African studies and less to the inherited historical and humanistic studies of the arts, letters, and philosophy from Western Europe. They want a "modern African education" for their future citizens, but the meaning of this phrase is seldom made very specific. Finally, they recognize that despite all the efforts they can put forward on their own initiative they will need for a long time to come an expanding supply of expatriate teachers, not fewer but more than they have had in the past; and they are needed at all educational levels.

These in briefest terms are some of the goals set by the developing countries themselves. I shall not try to judge here how realistic or how visionary such goals are.

But it *is* clear that any over-all planning for educational assistance and development in the transitional societies must take into account the hopes and aspirations of the new nations themselves, the interests of the more developed nations who are being asked to assist, and the effectiveness of the international agencies that embrace both. But it should also take into account what is often sadly lacking; namely, the needs of education itself and the knowledge about international education that is developing. Much of the talk about "national planning," "economic development," "investment in education," even "human resources development" is so impersonal that it does not seem to be very close to the millions of *individuals* whose lives and destinies are being affected. What then shall the educational profession of the world say to the national and international planners or developers of education on behalf of the children, students, and the adults who somehow get into the statistical tables, the flow charts, and the graphic models, simply as faceless "manpower requirements" or "human resources"? What shall we say about the *kind* of education required for the *human* development of the people of those nations that would be both modern and free?

[2] UNESCO, Conference of African States on the Development of Education in Africa, "Outline of a Plan for African Education Development," *Final Report* (Addis Ababa: May 15–25, 1961), Chapter III, p. 11.

On their behalf let me pose some sample questions that the youth of any country might well put to their educational planners:

1. Yes, by all means, we do want an education for economic development. We do want to learn the skills and the techniques of earning a better living whether we stay in the villages or whether we go to the cities. We do want to study those things that will enable us to increase gross national production and thus contribute to the improvement of life for all of our people as well as for ourselves. But do you want us to concentrate on the sciences and technical studies or shall we also gain a general education by study of the humanities and social sciences? Will you help us to plan our personal lives in relation to national goals, or will you simply assign us to various schools on the basis of tests you may give us? Will you build incentives for us as well as build buildings for us? Will you ask all of us who are to be educated at the advanced levels to serve our country, say by a period of rural service or community development or teaching in the schools, as well as to acquire specific skills and training? Yes, we want an education for economic development, but we want and need much more.

2. If you teach us to revel, as we now do, in no longer being ruled by those who are alien to our soil, will you also teach us how to govern ourselves? Will you teach us how to be good citizens and take our part in the political process and choose good leaders? Will you teach those of us still in the villages how to communicate with our brethren who have gone off to the cities or off to Europe and America and have returned an education that has opened their eyes but not ours? In the interest of national unity will you teach us how to curb our own special or particular loyalties and how to get along with our neighbors and fellow citizens even though their language, or their race, or their politics, or their religion, or perhaps all of these together are different from ours and therefore somewhat alien to us? Will you teach us the hard and real meaning of freedom as well as the exultation at being independent of foreign rule?

3. If you are going to change our lives drastically, as you plan to do, if you are going to create within us new wants and new aspirations for material and political things, and if you are going to change the traditional forms of society which have given us a kind of psychological security even if not very much physical security, will you also teach us how to live in a society that is moving rapidly from traditional ways of behaving to modern ways? Will you teach us a modern style of life? If you teach us to read and urge us to be more active in economic as well as political affairs, will you also teach us how to live as a "modern" person in a society that is not yet modern? We may lose a sense of who we are in all

this change. Will you help us to find a new personal identity as well as to feel a part of a new national identity? And will you do this for our sake and our self-fulfillment rather than for yours?

4. And if you teach us, as we are glad to learn, that our own past and our own culture and our own peoples are worthy of respect and pride, and if we learn in school or university more about our own race and culture and inherited wisdom rather than so much about the arts and sciences of the advanced nations of the Western world, and if we learn these things in our own languages rather than in imported languages, will you also teach us how to keep in touch with other nations, how to play our responsible role in the international community of nations, how to act as though we were the powerful world leaders, and how to make our contributions to the peace and security of the world?

5. And, finally, if you are going to keep on asking for teachers to come from other lands to help man our schools and universities, when are you going to teach us how to educate ourselves? Will you give special thought to training more of us as teachers, and will you try to keep us in the teaching profession so that we can become the main regenerative force in educating future generations of our people without having to rely so heavily upon outside assistance? And, above all, will you give us the kind of education and teacher training that will enable us to put into practice the answers to the questions that we have just been putting to you?

I am glad that I do not have to answer such questions as these, and obviously they have not been phrased in the language of the primary school child. But I do believe that it is the responsibility of the professional educators both within and outside of particular national borders to ask such questions as these on behalf of the children and adults of the nations of the world. The professional educator with his responsibility to the international community of scholarship and education cannot with impunity leave education solely to the political planners, or to the economic planners, or to the military planners—or to the academic planners. They are not so likely to be concerned about the individual destinies of the persons involved as are the educators whose job it is to have just that concern. It is true, of course, that educators within each country and among different countries do not all have the same ideas as to what is best for the welfare of the children and students, but that simply makes the task harder for the planners and requires that the planners and the educators work more closely together—for the sake of the persons affected.

Let me now make one or two points about each of the questions I have put to the national planners and also refer in the most general terms to the possible contribution of American development educators and teachers to each.

EDUCATION FOR ECONOMIC DEVELOPMENT

I shall not try to sort out the arguments among the economists as to what precise role education can play in speeding up the economic growth of nations. No matter what econometrics the economists use, it is clear that they have come more and more to the belief that expansion of education *does* have a significant role to play in economic development.

It may seem obvious to say that education in science and technical and vocational education are better for economic growth than are the humanities or arts. But I find even some economists saying that a balanced *general* education is more important than strictly technical education in the secondary schools and that much specific vocational training should go on in the employing institutions rather than in the schools. Others put the stress on the role of primary education in improving the agriculture and the conditions of rural life as the strategic place to concentrate, never mind the purely academic type of European-imported education. And still others would stress the importance of building up the practical or professional bias in secondary and higher education in order to overcome inherited antipathies to manual work and to managerial, technical, industrial, and commercial occupations as compared with the advantages of government service.

Still I find an overwhelming consensus among international economists who have written on this subject recently that the building of human resources is the greatest need of the least modern societies and that education offered in formal institutions, training offered in

employing institutions, and the building of incentives[3] are fundamental to this process. So much has been written about the value of
investment in education as a means of economic development that I
shall stress only one point.

Teachers are stressed over and over again as the key to building
human resources. While this may have been obvious to those of us in
professional education, it is good to know that teachers are now considered to be indispensable by the economists who have long been
preoccupied with capital, money, and the production and distribution
of goods as the essential elements in economic growth. It is refresh-
ing to find Frederick H. Harbison proposing, for example:

> The manpower assessment would probably also suggest that, in a coun-
> try committed to accelerated growth (with emphasis on industrialisation
> and modernization of agriculture), at least half of the students at both
> the intermediate and university levels should concentrate on technical
> subjects such as science, engineering, medicine, agriculture, veterinary
> medicine or pharmacy. Another 25 per cent should go to intermediate-
> level teacher-training colleges, and the remainder would concentrate on
> law, letters, social sciences, and business administration.[4]

One can perhaps quarrel with Harbison's "quotas," but my point is
that teachers are desperately needed and needed now, especially expatriate teachers for the secondary schools, for the teacher training
colleges, and for the universities. I am convinced that such American
programs as TEA, the Peace Corps, and educational development by
AID in building institutions of teacher training are providing the
most important kinds of international educational assistance directed
at economic development that the United States can provide to less
developed nations. But the potential of their usefulness and influence
cannot be limited to economic matters.

[3] For an interesting theory of the sources of the "need for achievement" and
its role in economic development, see David C. McClelland, *The Achieving
Society* (Princeton, N.J.: Van Nostrand Co., Inc., 1961).

[4] Frederick H. Harbison, *Human Resources Development Planning in Mod-
ernising Economies*, Inter-University Study of Labor Problems in Economic Development, Reprint No. 29 (Reprinted for private circulation from *International
Labour Review*, LXXXV, No. 5, May 1962), p. 18.

EDUCATION FOR SELF-GOVERNMENT

Fortunately, modernization is now being recognized as largely a political process, not simply economic. Fortunately, too, political scientists have recently joined economists in their concern for analyzing and studying the developmental process of the new nations. A good deal of interesting work is being produced in this field. A notable example is *The Politics of the Developing Areas*, which contains chapters by Gabriel A. Almond of Yale and James S. Coleman of the University of California at Los Angeles, as well as Lucian W. Pye of M.I.T., Myron Weiner of Chicago, Dankwart A. Rustow of Columbia, and George I. Blanksten of Northwestern.[5]

There is much of importance for education in their attempt to develop a theory of political systems appropriate to non-Western cultures and to classify the political systems of African, Asian, and Latin American countries at various stages of development from traditional oligarchy through modernizing oligarchy to political democracy. There is also much of interest for education in the hypothesis that there is a correlation between economic development and political systems whereby in general the more competitive the political system the more active is the economic development, and the more authoritarian the political system the lower are the indices of economic development. The usual indices of development include not only several items having to do with per capita wealth, industrialization, and urbanization, but also the per cent of literacy in the population and the per cent of children actually enrolled in primary schools. I hope that one day we shall be able to arrive at some valid empirical generalizations concerning the *kind* of education, not simply the *amount*, that contributes most effectively to economic and political development.

There has been in past political theory too great polarization between the so-called traditional political systems and the modern

[5] Gabriel A. Almond and James S. Coleman (eds.), *The Politics of the Developing Areas* (Princeton, N.J.: Princeton University Press, 1960). The book and the research involved in it were jointly sponsored by the Princeton Center of International Studies and the Committee on Comparative Politics of the Social Science Research Council.

states. Almond and Coleman and their colleagues are arguing that all political systems have certain features of structure and function in common and that all political systems exhibit a mixture of traditional and modern forms: The primary, informal, interpersonal, face-to-face relationships so characteristic of traditional societies also operate in a modern system as well; even though the secondary relationships of formal, legal, impersonal, objective, and functionally specific relationships do dominate a modern system. The real difference, they argue, is that in a modern system the secondary structures have greater control over the primary relationships (a Western parliamentarian is likely to be, or ought to be, more loyal to parliamentary forms than to his family relationships), whereas in the non-Western systems the formal rules more often give way to the informal ties of family, caste, or class.

Thus schools and educational institutions should help each new generation of youth to "domesticate" the informal relationships of family or tribe and learn to live according to the new demands of modern political nationhood which are based upon modern practices of political and party organization and modern standards of governmental performance in public administration. Education must be devoted to induction into general citizenship whether this be called "political socialization and recruitment" or widespread "political participation." The youth and adults of the new nations, as of all free nations, must gain knowledge about the working of a modern governmental system in which the powers of legislation, of administration, and of judicial appeal are exercised with a degree of separation or independence or "boundary maintenance," but they must also learn the new roles expected of free citizens in an independent state. If they are to develop "democratic forms" or "competitive political systems," they must learn how to behave in political parties that genuinely attempt to represent the interests and demands of various associational groups as these are organized for functionally specific purposes in the society. They must learn "political roles and behavior" throughout the political process including the role of a loyal and coherent opposition party.

I do not believe that schools can take for granted that the tremendously important transition from traditional to modern political systems will automatically take place or that it should be left solely to the political leaders, political parties, or agencies of mass communication. I can only believe that schools and universities must play a political role both in classroom study and in the whole life of the school. I cannot believe therefore that the social sciences should automatically find a subordinate place in the curriculum of modernizing nations or that self-government activities of schools should be neglected as learning experiences. The most serious attention should be given by the new nations to this problem. It is probably no accident that extremist political ideas and unruly extremist student behavior accompany the neglect of objective and candid study of the social sciences in the curriculum of so many secondary schools and universities in many parts of the world. But we need careful studies of this problem too.

I know that this is a touchy subject, I know the dangers of political manipulation in the social science field, and I know how cautious outsiders must be in doing anything that could appear to be interfering in the politics of another nation. But surely there must be some way in which self-government can be learned by oncoming generations without political manipulation *and* with outside help. I know of no better reliance than upon serious, sustained, objective study of basic political matters under the guidance of fair-minded teachers who take as their authority the best scholarly evidence and research that can be marshaled on the crucial issues facing the responsible leaders and intellectuals of a nation. If an objective, neutral, and autonomous system of communications is necessary for the development of an active and effective citizenship, how much more so is the necessity for formal and informal education to assist in the creation of "an informed stratum of citizens" who are "public policy-oriented, rather than interest-oriented in the narrow sense."[6]

Howard Wriggins of the Foreign Affairs Division, Legislative

6 *Ibid.*, p. 48.

Reference Service of the Library of Congress takes a similar point of view on this matter:

The educational system is of great importance for developing values and practices of political behavior. It can contribute significantly to the conception political leaders and masses have of the good society, of where they themselves are moving and how best to reach their goal. The political values taught in the classrooms, the political convictions or argumentation of the teachers, the effect of the mode of teaching on the personalities of the children and their attitudes toward authority and dissent, and the practice provided in the schools and universities for experimenting with responsibility and the management of small controversies in a serious manner—all these and more elements in the educational experience are of importance to the socialization of young people into the modes and values of political life.

These aspects of the educational system go far beyond the technical education American assistance programs have tended to strengthen, although efforts to teach inventiveness and innovation in the technological line probably affect attitudes of students toward dealing with other aspects of life as well. Indeed, the more technological specialization, the more likely are students to become impatient with traditional social ways, but this in itself will not provide political skills or judgment for constructively changing these ways.

. . . there may be many ways in which the United States can, with tact and understanding, assist in curricular instruction and extracurricular activities. The aim should be to bring the educational system closer to the needs of the country; provide the type of skills which give young people real opportunities to exercise their talents in improving their own societies when they leave school or college; and encourage those values that lead to a sharing of power and responsibility, increased empathy toward other groups, broader participation in making decisions, and easier collaboration with peers.[7]

Educational planners will also face the problem of developing national loyalties among the diverse racial, linguistic, ethnic, and religious groups which so often characterize the nations undergoing rapid transition. Somehow the common loyalties to the nation will need to rise above the particularist or separatist loyalties that are so tempting to many politicians to exploit for their personal gain or

[7] Howard Wriggins, "Foreign Assistance and Political Development," *Development of the Emerging Countries; An Agenda for Research* (Washington, D.C.: The Brookings Institution, 1962), pp. 209–210.

power. Informal, particularistic, primary groups based on lineage, caste, language, religion, urban or rural cleavages, or regional loyalty may demand their own schools in order to perpetuate their "communal" interests. What then shall be the answer? Should they be permitted to have their own schools; indeed, should they be encouraged to do so by receiving financial assistance and teachers from the government? Or should government schools open freely to all children of all groups be the predominant pattern of the future? The relative values of a common public school system in contrast to a system of separatist or particularist schools may turn out to be one of the most difficult problems for the new educational planners—as it has long been in the United States.

Many countries are being torn by two drives—one, to use education as a means of building national unity among diverse racial, ethnic, religious, and linguistic groups; the other, the drive of the different groups to demand separate schools to cultivate their own language, religion, ethnic customs, or political outlook. Division among groups leads to demands for separate schools; and the separate schools tend in turn to perpetuate the divisions, perhaps to delay unification as a nation, or even to delay independence itself.

Educational planners in many countries are thus faced with this question: What kind of educational system will enable us to overcome group divisions and separatist tendencies and build a unified nation in which people can live under laws and institutions devoted to justice but at the same time will encourage the diversity and the flexibility that will enable individuals and diverse groups to develop themselves and to live in conditions of security, dignity, and freedom?

Finally, the problem of learning self-government is, of course, larger than the narrowly political. It has to do with the whole process of learning to behave in new kinds of organizations of all kinds:

With respect to political development, it is apparent that we cannot think simply in terms of a quantitative decline in traditional role characteristics and a rise in modern ones. We must consider instead what mixture, or rather fusion, of traditional and modern patterns will lead to national development. . . .

These considerations suggest that it may be fruitful to think of the problems of development and modernization as rooted in the need to create more effective, more adaptive, more complex, and more rationalized organizations.[8]

It now appears that the modern, formal superstructure of relationships can give an organization strength only if supported by the powerful emotional forces arising from particularistic loyalties and by the cohesive powers of the endlessly complex but functionally diffuse sentiments that human beings can provoke in each other.[9]

We have gone into some detail to suggest the importance of the informal, highly personal, and what are customarily considered to be traditional forms of behavior in order to counter the idea that development is merely the strengthening of the more formal, more legalistic, and more narrowly functionally relevant patterns of behavior. The development of effective organizations depends fundamentally upon the capacity of individuals to associate with each other. This capacity calls into question a wide range of basic human values and the ability of individuals to make commitments—commitments as to the goals and purposes of group action, the means and spirit of associational relationships, the appropriate limits of such associations and the integrity of the self; in short, commitments as to one's fundamental identity both as a member of human societies (and subsocieties) and as an individual.[10]

The several relationships between a teacher and his pupils in their firsthand contacts with one another both inside and outside the classroom can be the means of learning how to behave and how to develop the associational skills required in new kinds of organizations. In a genuine sense, then, the classroom and the playing field with their personal contact between teacher and pupil are "traditional" forms of association that can be most effective as the foundation upon which the superstructure of modernizing legal, political and economic organizations may rest. I do not see how the new technology of education, film strips, radio, television, or teaching machines, can provide this "fusion" of the traditional personal forms with the modern impersonal forms except as supplementary aids to the personal relationships of the classroom.

[8] Pye, op. cit., p. 38.
[9] Ibid., p. 40.
[10] Ibid., p. 41.

And this indeed may be where the American TEA or Peace Corps teacher is at his best, if he has developed professional skill and understanding of the processes of human development and personality growth of his pupils. Simple knowledge of subject matter is not enough. It may be that the American teachers' sense for the personal and the *informal* in the sense of giving affective and emotional support to pupils, their concerns, and their interests, if bulwarked by sound academic knowledge and professional understanding, can be one of the most effective aids to the youth of new lands who are seeking to move from traditional to modern ways of life.

EDUCATION FOR A MODERN STYLE OF LIFE

The psychological problem involved in the transition from traditional to modern modes of life may be much more difficult to deal with than the purely economic or political. A number of recent studies have begun to give increasing attention to the problem. For example, Daniel Lerner argues that the modern personal style in contrast to the traditional is the "mobile personality" marked by empathy; that is, "the capacity to see oneself in the other fellow's situation."

It is a major hypothesis of this study that high empathic capacity is the predominant personal style only in modern society, which is distinctively industrial, urban, literate and *participant*. Traditional society is nonparticipant—it deploys people by kinship into communities isolated from each other and from a center; without an urban-rural division of labor, it develops few needs requiring economic interdependence; lacking the bonds of interdependence, people's horizons are limited by locale and their decisions involve only other *known* people in *known* situations. Hence, there is no need for a transpersonal common doctrine formulated in terms of shared secondary symbols—a national "ideology" which enables persons unknown to each other to engage in political controversy or achieve "consensus" by comparing their opinions. Modern society is participant in that it functions by "consensus"—individuals making personal decisions on public issues must concur often enough with other individuals they do not know to make possible a stable common governance. Among the marks of this historic achievement in social organization, which we call Participant Society, are that most people go through school, read newspapers, receive cash payments in jobs they are legally free to change, buy goods for cash in an open market, vote in elections which actually decide among competing candidates, and express opinions on many matters which are not their personal business.

Especially important, for the Participant Style, is the enormous proportion of people who are expected to "have opinions" on public matters—and the corollary expectation of these people that their opinions will matter. It is this subtly complicated structure of reciprocal expectation which sustains widespread empathy.[11]

Think for a moment how important the expatriate teacher can be in helping students in transitional societies to see themselves in "the other fellow's position." Think how important the expatriate teacher can be in firsthand portrayal day-by-day of "the other fellow." I have seen this being done with skill both by TEA and Peace Corps teachers. As teachers display disciplined and carefully thought out "opinions on public matters," they can become primary agents for inducting the young of a neo-traditional society into a modern style of life. The expatriate teacher must not get involved in the politics of a host country, but still the educational process itself is concerned with learning how to think about the issues raised in the subject matter at hand. A great deal of careful study and investigation is needed if this aspect of education for modernity in transitional societies is to be given the attention it deserves.

The problem is put by Max F. Millikan this way:

Perhaps the most pervasive element in the modernization process is the profound and progressive widening of men's perceptions of the realistic alternatives open to them, sometimes referred to as the revolution of rising expectations. Too frequently the term has been used as if it referred exclusively to expectations in the economic sense, to newly perceived possibilities of consumption and standards of living which in traditional societies men would have regarded as wholly unattainable. Such new perceptions do indeed exist, but there are also more profound and far-reaching changes in men's views of the world and of the individual's place in it. Men begin seriously to contemplate new values, new forms of political organization, new kinds of careers, new access to knowledge, new relations with those who have traditionally been their superiors, their in-

[11] Daniel Lerner, *The Passing of Traditional Society* (Glencoe, Ill.: The Free Press, 1958), pp. 50–51.

feriors, and their peers. They perceive new patterns of social organization, new possibilities of movement, new kinds of leisure.

The pace varies, but this widening of perceived alternatives is universal and inevitable. Three forces tend to start it and keep it moving: widened contact and communication with more modern societies, the rise of trade and of cities, and the emergence of new generations born into a world where modern activity is increasingly a fact of life rather than a perceived break with the past. The widening of perceptions occurs first among a limited element of the elite of the society, especially those exposed through education, government, or commerce to life outside the traditional society. It gradually spreads to wider segments of the population until it becomes a popular rather than an elite phenomenon; and today there is almost no backward segment of the most traditional society which has not been to some degree touched by this process, though its more massive consequences still lie ahead.[12]

Again, the teacher and especially the sensitive expatriate teacher can be most significant in the process of "widening men's perceptions." I have seen TEA teachers spend most of a class period in helping the students fill in cultural background and meanings so that the lesson being studied could have more significance for the students than the mere recitations of words in a foreign language.

Finally, on this theme, I am particularly impressed by the eloquent analysis of Lucian W. Pye. Pointing to the personal insecurities of people caught up in this radical change so often covered up by the essentially bland term "development," he observes:

This is also a time of personal insecurity, for millions must make frightening adjustments in their personal perspectives on life. Never has the extent of basic social change touched the lives of so many, shaking the intellectual, moral, and emotional foundations of their individual worlds. In addition to suffering the pain and discomfort of being torn from the old and the known, they are confronted with the most basic of human issues, that of individual integrity and personal identity. For the old is, above all, that which both friend and foe must use without hesitation or qualification to define the uniqueness of the self, of the "we" which is the essence of identity in the human community; and the new is seen by friend and foe alike as the essence of that which is unmistakably the foreign, the West, the "they." The logic of tragedy underlies the psychological travail of millions as they seek to adjust to the new, because the

12 Millikan and Blackmer, op. cit., pp. 94–95.

"they" of the new once conquered or dominated or belittled the "we" of the old.

Most disturbing of all, the "they," the West, with insensitivity and unfathomable motives, has zealously offered self-sacrificing assistance to make the "we" more like the "they." The insensitivity of the helping "they," whether appearing in the guise of the earlier champions of the "white man's burden" or of the latter-day ideologues of economic development, comes from the blinding effects of their possessing a correct historical perspective. To them, since change is inevitable, it can only be temporarily painful; it cannot be appreciated as being psychologically intolerable. The motives of the "they" are beyond comprehension—and hence are disturbing—for even the decision makers of the West cannot tell what mixture of self-interest and self-sacrifice, of hard calculation and human charity, have inspired their acts. American policy makers, for example, need to reassure themselves repeatedly that foreign aid is only an expression of enlightened self-interest and not an act of charity for less fortunate peoples, but they become irate whenever the recipients of such aid tell them that this is precisely the way it is.[13]

Nothing can do more to allay haunting uncertainties, doubts about motives, and mutual suspicions than the day-to-day transaction between a dedicated teacher and his inquiring students. In the search for identity the expatriate teacher and the "patriate" student are both in search of their identities. Each can help the other. The transitional student needs a feeling of predictability, something, or someone he can count on and trust. The expatriate teacher also needs to find his own purpose in being there.

Pye sums up what must be the predicament of many African students:

First, there is the problem of certainty or predictability: people in transitional societies can take almost nothing for granted; they are plagued on all sides by uncertainty and every kind of unpredictable behavior. In their erratically changing world, every relationship rests upon uncertain foundations and may seem to contain an unlimited potential for good or evil. People are not sure what they should get from any relationship, and so they are never sure whether they are getting what they should. The concepts of friend and foe become blurred. Above all else, the individual cannot be sure about the actions of others because he cannot be sure about himself.

[13] Pye, op. cit., p. 4.

Second, there is the related problem of a lack of trust in human relationships. The problem is broader and deeper than just the prevalence
of distrust among individuals. It colors people's feelings about their relationship to their surrounding world, to the unfolding of events, and it
affects their time perspective. The feeling of basic distrust leaves people
unsure of their control over their world and hence fearful that the world is
either against them or indifferent to them. Distrusting others, they must
distrust their own capacity to influence others, and hence they have feelings of impotence. Unsure about the meaning of events, they are prone to
distrust time, to believe that dreaming is dangerous and that nothing good
is likely to come out of the future.[14]

Conversely, the teacher himself may begin to find his own identity
in the task of providing the kind of guidance and trust only a good
teacher can provide:

There is an immense need for education. There is a need for teachers.
I have seldom felt as if I was engaged in work for which the need was
more apparent. I feel that the work I am doing is worthwhile. The
young men whom I teach will take important positions in government
and in the service of their country and peoples. Nothing gives me more
pleasure than knowing that I am contributing to their education and that
the impact of their lives will have profound effects upon the future of
these lands.

I feel that my powers are being fully engaged because of the delicate
and sensitive nature of the mission. I am not an instrument of political
persuasion. I hope that my students will learn to think and be free. They
must find solutions based upon independent inquiry. They must arrive at
answers for what best suits their individual and unique destiny. This is
why the mission is delicate and sensitive.

The challenge to be versatile and to exercise the imagination is unlimited. Because this is the beginning there are countless opportunities
for using present talents, and countless demands to cultivate new powers.
The teacher in these lands must, in fact, be prepared to accept these demands. . . .

It is good for us to be here, if only that we may begin to understand
the immense problems and invest these lands through contributions to
education with a steady faith in the ultimate success of the future. The
virtues of the moment are praise not blame, calm not passion, and
sympathy with and pride in the brave attempt.[15]

[14] *Ibid.*, pp. 54–55.
[15] From a letter written by a member of the Teachers for East Africa Project
now teaching in Kenya, Nathaniel Frothingham III, Harvard '61.

EDUCATION FOR INTERNATIONAL RESPONSIBILITY

We in the United States have known the desirability and the satisfactions of gaining political independence and attaining a high degree of freedom of thought and action. And we are just coming to know what it means to be an indissoluble part of the world. We have been forced to move rapidly from isolation and neutralism to world leadership, and we are still trying to learn how to think and act accordingly. But this means that we know what other still newer nations are going through. We cannot be too impatient with their longing for isolation or neutralism, but at the same time we can hope and expect sooner or later that all nations will act as though they too were world leaders upon whose policies, outlook, and action the peace and security of the entire world might depend.

Surely, education in the new nations must more quickly take account of the wider world than did our own. Education in all nations must be concerned with the worldwide development of people as well as with the economic and political development of nations. The new nations despite their legitimate concerns to develop studies appropriate to themselves are no exception to this principle. The essence of modernity (among many other essences) is to be inevitably a part of the whole world. Only the most hopelessly traditional of societies can hope to remain isolated and cut off from international responsibility.

Much, therefore, of what I have had to say about the three stages of international education in America will apply to the new nations. It would be a pity if the new nations turned their backs on international studies in education just at a time when the older nations are discovering the importance of knowledge and understanding of other peoples. In fact the new nations could benefit from having expatriate teachers—an excellent means of participating in international education and cultural exchange without leaving home. The expatriate teachers should thus be "exploited" as their pupils seek to learn as much as they can about the life and culture from which the teachers come.

The new nations are quite right in wanting to redress the imbalance in their inherited academic curriculum in which local history and culture were neglected in favor of a fairly pure importation of European history, literature, arts, and science. As this imbalance is corrected and as African and Asian studies are given greater emphasis, it may well be that the *international* aspects of the social sciences and humanities should also be broadened and strengthened rather than reduced. The trouble has been not that European history has been taught, but that it has been taught from a narrowly European point of view and often focused upon one or two European nations. European history should not be given up simply in order to stress African or Asian history. African and Asian history should be emphasized in the setting of *world* history. Literature should be studied—or rejected—because of its literary quality, not just because it happened to be English, American, French, Russian, Indian, or Chinese. Excellence should be the criterion for studying literature or art—no matter what part of the world it comes from.

I know that this may sound like hollow preaching to ears that have heard little or no praise for local or national talent; nevertheless, all nations must face up to the fact that the future character of the international community is of over-riding importance to us all. We must all learn to become more receptive in the presence of a developing "world culture":

Although nation building is essentially a domestic process, it comes about in response to international forces. Indeed, the concept of the nation-state and the standards of modern state behavior have little meaning except within the context of a world-wide nation-state system. Societies throughout history have generated change, and the cultures have mingled; the distinctive character of social change in the new countries of today is that it is occurring largely in response to the diffusion of what we may call a world culture based upon modern science and technology, modern practices of organization, and modern standards of governmental performance. It is helpful to think of all of these elements of the modern world as representing a culture, for from the point of view of the society as a whole or of the individual personality they are related to each other in much the same coherent fashion as the elements of a culture are felt to be. The concept of culture is also helpful in that it suggests that there may be an inner logic to the process of change and that the act of be-

coming a part of the modern world is in essence a process of acculturation.[16]

The new nations of the world could lead the way for all of us if
they were to remodel their curriculums not narrowly by simply playing up their own national images (all of the "modern" nations have
done that), but by being the first to develop curriculums built upon
the emerging world culture as it affects them.

Finally, we could really make "educational assistance" a two-way
process if we could join together in helping to define through our
mutual educational efforts the nature of the international community
which will nourish all nations that would be modern and free. Think
of the leadership the professional educators of both traditional and
modern countries could exert if they agreed to work together in
the spirit of the following propositions by Lucian Pye:

> To overcome our uneasiness about speaking across the gap in culture
> and technology between our society and the underdeveloped countries
> we need to remind ourselves that a primary thrust behind the quest of
> transitional people is their vision of more just and more democratic ways
> of life. It is the democratic element within the world culture that con-
> tinues to have the greatest potency in moving men to act. To an extraor-
> dinary degree, and in the face of all the anxieties produced by the ac-
> culturation process, the transitional peoples have continually committed
> themselves to realizing democratic values and forms. . . . The degree to
> which legitimacy has already been related to some formulation of the
> democratic spirit in most of the newly emergent countries is truly im-
> pressive.
>
> If American policy is to be turned to the furtherance of democratic
> political development, the stage must be set for frank and candid discus-
> sions about fundamental political values. Given all the anxieties and in-
> securities produced by the acculturation process, this can be done only
> if we demonstrate a full commitment to associate ourselves for better or
> worse in assisting and strengthening those transitional peoples who
> would build democratic societies. By communicating our genuine con-
> cern and real respect for them and for their problems, we can produce a
> quality of relationship which will make it possible for us to confront to-
> gether fundamental issues. If we are prepared to commit ourselves truly
> to assisting in the task of nation building, we can provide sufficient re-

[16] Pye, op. cit., p. 10.

assurance to a transitional people to enable us both to break out of the falsely sentimental and unduly hypocritical moods that have surrounded so many of our associations in the past. In such a spirit of association it should also be possible for us to assist the acculturation process by sympathetically but rigorously pushing for exacting standards of performance. Without a basic sense of commitment in our relationship with the underdeveloped countries we shall either continue to find it impossible to apply hard and meaningful standards in granting our aid or we shall discover that our insistence upon standards will be seen as insulting and degrading.[17]

How better to "bridge the gap" between our culture and theirs than to have hundreds of teachers and thousands of students in daily and hourly contact over a period of years during which a mutual trust, reassurance, and respect can be built up on both sides. Upon the basis of such mutual confidence the candid dialogue concerning each others' problems and our respective roles in the world could surely follow. The beneficial effects might come more quickly than may be realized. If 5,000 American teachers each have 100 students in their classes, a half million of the most able young people in the world are touched annually. And the students will become amazingly soon the leaders of their countries.

American policy can perhaps make no greater contribution to the nation-building process than to give transitional people confidence that there is now emerging a strong international community in which they can find their national destinies and achieve self-respect and genuine acceptance for what they are as human beings.

Possibly we can also assist people in purely political matters to a far greater extent than we appreciate. For different reasons, both Westerners and the leaders of the new countries have tended to shy away from the fundamental issues in nation building, preferring to talk about supposedly innocuous technical and administrative matters than about politics. Nation building is above all else a political matter, which means that at the heart of the problem lie questions of values of human trust, and of the proper sharing of power. In destroying the world of traditional societies, the West forced the emerging countries to confront profound issues about fundamental values; the West should not now try to retreat into innocent discussions about impersonal technical and economic mat-

17 *Ibid.,* p. 300.

ters. We should rather be projecting through all of our actions the vision of a just world order composed of new political societies.[18]

And how can "American policy" convey this confidence more effectively than by the example of hundreds of American teachers and educators displaying in person that America really believes in a "benign international system"? How can we better "project through all our actions the vision of a just world order" than by the fair-minded, rigorously objective, scholarly treatment by TEA and Peace Corps teachers of the fundamental problems that the peoples of the world must face candidly and resolutely? The social science teachers do this as they deal with the basic problems of nation building and international relations (not "politics" in the narrow sense); science and mathematics teachers display the objectivity and skill required of a professional in all modern societies; and English teachers aid in acquiring competence in one of the important international languages of the world. As the democratic ideal shines through all that our international teachers and advisers do, they will aid other peoples not only to build themselves into new nations but into a new and responsible kind of "international nationhood" which could even become a model for the older and more modern nations to emulate.

EDUCATION FOR THE REGENERATION OF EDUCATION

Just as a nation that would be modern and free must develop a measure of self-sustaining economic growth, must become self-governing to a marked degree, and must acquire the sensibilities and outlooks required by the modern world and international community, so must it develop the means whereby its own educational system becomes largely self-sustaining. A modern and free nation must have within itself the power to generate and regenerate the needed educational development that will serve its people well. A modern and free nation cannot rely indefinitely upon other nations for its teachers. To generate its own education it must produce its own teachers. Teacher education thus becomes one of the most urgent needs of the emergent nations.

[18] *Ibid.*, pp. 299–300.

The goal is simply stated. All the new nations have to do is to provide an excellent academic and professional training for a greatly increased number of persons who will be competent to build an educational system devoted to economic development, self government, a modern style of life, and international responsibility and who will be willing to devote their lives to teaching in overcrowded classrooms with inadequate instructional aids for long hours, for low pay, and with little public esteem.

To put the goal this way is, of course, unfair. But I do so to indicate that the problem is a vast and formidable one for any nation to face, even those that presumably have plenty of money. This is why the emerging nations are determined to devote more to educational expenditure than some economists think they should. It is why they grasp at the idea that the new technology can do the job more quickly, more effectively, and more cheaply while at the same time reducing the number of teachers needed for expanding primary or secondary education. It is why they are trying to experiment with shorter periods of academic or professional training for new teachers than has been the case in their highly selective systems of education. It is why they seek the aid of teachers from outside to help keep their systems going until the self-sustaining generator known as teacher training can begin to produce the number of teachers they need.

But the problem in many countries is still more complicated than this. The inherited educational traditions of most nations of the world give more prestige and more salary and thus require more educational attainment of their secondary school teachers than they do of their primary school teachers. Generally speaking, the secondary school deals with that small minority of the population that is headed for the university, and the secondary school teacher is often required to have a university degree as well as professional training acquired at university level.

In contrast, the primary school teacher is not required and in most cases not permitted to attend a university, and in some countries he will not even have attended a secondary school. But he regularly will have attended a teacher training college devoted specifically to the training of teachers for the primary schools. The training college course may be parallel to the secondary school course, in which case it is likely to be lower in prestige than the secondary school and to attract students of somewhat lower academic quality and lower social status. Or the teacher training college course may follow the secondary school and be parallel to the degree granting institutions (though not be one) in which case it will be lower in prestige and may well attract students of lower academic quality and lower social status than would be true of those who attend the universities.

Only rarely is it possible in such countries for a person who has attended a teacher training college to go on to a university; the reason is that he will rarely have attended a secondary school or have passed secondary school examinations at a high enough level. On the other hands, students who have the ability and the opportunity to pass the examinations of the secondary school and do go through the university and acquire a degree too often do not want to teach. The opportunity for advancement open to a university graduate, especially in the newly independent countries of Africa, is so great that a person with a degree often prefers to go into government service or into another professional service than to teach in the secondary schools; a university graduate would seldom think of teaching in a primary school.

Many countries are thus faced with the problem of recruitment and incentive for their teachers: How can they enlist the talents of their able young people for the field of teaching and then keep them committed to teaching once they are enlisted? How can the primary school teacher be kept in the field of teaching while still enabled to progress further in his academic and professional qualifications in order to improve the quality of the primary schools? And how can the university graduate be enlisted in the field of teaching and given such professional satisfaction that he will devote himself to the education of his countrymen and forsake the glamor or power of immediate government service?

Another example of the problems facing teacher education has to

·do with the relation of government to the training colleges on one hand and to the universities on the other hand. Governments often feel that the training of teachers, especially of primary school teachers, is *their* province and that therefore the ministries of education should exert direct control over the teacher training colleges, while the universities feel that the training of secondary school teachers is *their* province and that the ministries of education should not meddle too much.

In countries that have a tradition of belief in the autonomy of universities and at the same time are relying more and more upon government to speed up educational and social change, there is likely to be a clash between government and university over teacher training; or each will simply go its own way—the government continuing to run teacher training institutions which are divorced academically and professionally from the universities. I do not have the answer to this problem, but it is an extremely important one: How can the teacher training colleges and the universities legitimately serve the needs of a newly independent country and still preserve the kinds of autonomy and freedom which are internationally recognized as essential to the pursuit of knowledge and to a rationally based academic life?

There are still other problems that plague the training of teachers in many countries. For example, the educational tradition in the upper secondary forms and at the universities has been one of intense specialization. Students begin to specialize in science or mathematics or the arts in the upper years of the secondary school and then pursue further specialization at the university level. Several of the countries are beginning to experiment with a greater emphasis upon general education. They see this as especially desirable for teachers who often need to teach several subjects, not just one, and who also need the power and insight to generalize from one idea or body of knowledge to another. But the strong tradition of specialization is going to make it very difficult for the idea of general education to take hold.

Another tradition has been one of great emphasis at the secondary and university level on the academic, theoretical subjects and a relative neglect of the more technical, practical, or professional studies. Since preferment in government and professional service has been based upon achievement in academic examinations, the academic subjects have been preferred by the more able students; but now there is a growing feeling that countries which would change themselves rapidly in a technological as well as a social way must give more attention to the technical, scientific, and professional studies. Again, this is easier said than done.

Still another problem is the relatively inferior academic status conferred upon the social sciences within the hierarchy of academic studies. In some countries science and mathematics have had the highest prestige. In others it has been the humanities and the Western European classics. Despite the fact that many countries neglect the social sciences in favor of either the sciences or the humanities, there now is a movement in some countries to put more stress upon such social sciences as history, political science, sociology, anthropology, economics, and geography as a means of widening the horizons and preventing a narrow kind of provincialism or exaggerated nationalism as these nations take their places front and center upon the world scene.

A final example of a common academic tradition particularly affects teacher training. At the university level the training of teachers for secondary schools is likely to be largely academic in content up to the first degree, leaving an exclusively professional education to the years beyond the first degree, whereas the training for primary school teachers in teacher training colleges is heavily methodological; in some cases it even fails to provide the teacher with the elements of a secondary school education. Interesting new plans are developing within several countries—plans that involve training for secondary school teachers in advanced but non-degree-granting training colleges as well as in university courses that will include the study of professional education within the first degree (B.Ed. or B.A. in Ed.).

I see merit in fundamental experimentation that looks toward the enhancement of general education as well as specialization, of professional and technical education that goes along with academic education, and the cultivation of those social sciences that will promote an objective and international perspective. As the new nations give careful attention to the kind of education that will serve them best in the years to come, I hope that they will regard the improvement of the quality of teachers and of teacher training institutions as a central task.

I have hopes that continuing international efforts of universities which represent diverse academic and professional traditions can overcome the obstacles I have just recited and can lead to the design and development of new programs and institutions of teacher education that will genuinely meet the needs of different developing countries. I believe that there is no more important task to which external aid efforts and the emerging peoples together can devote themselves than the building of better teacher training institutions. One such promising international enterprise is described in the Carnegie *Quarterly* as follows:

A shortage of secondary schools is one of Africa's gravest educational problems, and at its heart—quite overshadowing even the lack of money and physical facilities—is a dearth of qualified teachers. Great efforts are being made to supply foreign teachers on an interim basis; both the Peace Corps and the Agency for International Development, to name only two American agencies, are supplying hundreds at this very moment. But these represent merely ad hoc measures; the essential long-term need is for strengthening of African teacher education.

Such strengthening is the goal of a major cooperative effort launched almost three years ago with the aid of a Carnegie grant. Dubbed the Afro-Anglo-American Program in Teacher Education and generally referred to as the A-A-A, it involves ten institutions: Teachers College, Columbia University; the Institute of Education, University of London; and the institute or department of education in Pius XII College (Basutoland), University of Ghana, Ahmadu Bello University (Nigeria), University of Ibadan (Nigeria), University of Nigeria, University College of Rhodesia and Nyasaland, University College of Sierra Leone, and Makerere University College (Uganda).

The basic idea was simply that it should be possible for an international group of universities, all deeply concerned with African educational problems, to work together in developing solutions to those problems. The solutions must be truly African; yet it appeared reasonable to assume that some practices which had proved valuable elsewhere would prove adaptable to meeting special African needs. This provided the rationale for involving British and American institutions. In the United States it meant pulling together and developing resources at Teachers College, where there was already interest in African education. . . .

The A-A-A program is based on quality rather than numbers. A small training program for Americans prepares them for educational service in Africa. . . .

The emphasis on teacher-training institutions is deliberate, for it is believed that the A-A-A program can make its greatest contribution through producing staff members for such institutions rather than secondary schools. In line with this belief, there is a training program for Africans who either already are, or are being groomed to be, staff members of teacher-training institutions. . . .

An informal exchange program among all the participating institutions sends staff members from one to another for lectures, teaching, and consultation. In addition, meetings on teacher education are held in Africa with representatives from African, British, and American educational institutions as well as international organizations.[19]

My final text of hope for teacher education is taken from Lucian Pye's stress upon the importance of the professional role in new nations. Contemplating what can be done to break down the psychological barriers and inhibitions that arise in developing countries as a result of their search for personal and national identity, he finds the reassurance and sense of accomplishment that come from meeting international professional standards can be most useful. This sense can be achieved by the creation, as he happily phrases it, of "communities of modernizers who would constitute islands of stability in an otherwise erratically changing world." This idea corresponds closely with what I was suggesting when I spoke of the TEA as an "international teaching college." This says so well what American educators and teachers, A-A-A, TEA, Peace Corps, and others who follow them could be doing if they themselves are effective professionals. They could be

[19] Carnegie Corporation of New York, *Quarterly*, XI, No. 2 (April 1963), pp. 3–4.

. . . assisting individuals as individuals to find their sense of identity through the mastery of demanding skills. By this approach national development would be furthered as ever-increasing numbers of competent people meet in their daily lives the exacting but also psychologically reassuring standards of professional performance basic to the modern world. The emergence and interaction of such people as they fulfill their professional activities would provide transitional societies with communities of modernizers who would constitute islands of stability in an otherwise erratically changing world. The establishment of such communities would provide the necessary environment in which the more ambitious transitional people could escape the paralyzing effects of feeling isolated and alone in the search for new identities.

What we are suggesting is that the test of profession may prove to be a means of overcoming many of the psychological ambivalences produced by the acculturation process. The concepts and standards of the modern professions can uniquely serve the dual functions of assisting the individual in realizing his potentialities while also providing the community with the skills and abilities necessary for national development. In nation building it is not just the society that needs modern skills; the people must also feel skilled in modern terms. As individuals, the intelligent and ambitious peoples of transitional societies can acquire the skills and competences appropriate to membership in the modern world and readily become the equals of citizens of industrial societies as teachers, lawyers, scientists, soldiers, and, yes, as administrators and politicians. They can achieve essentially modern standards even though their countries may still have inadequate school systems, undermanned legal professions, and militarily weak armies. If the test of individual identity is tied more to personal roles and less to national indices, the problem of becoming a citizen of the modern world is greatly reduced. . . .

The inescapable realities of relative national power can impress upon people the incorrect conclusion that they as individuals may be inferior to others. Only by meeting honest standards of competence can such people convince themselves that they are the equals of all others.

On the other hand, if people can experience in their professional lives the sense of accomplishment which comes from meeting meaningful and demanding standards, they are likely to realize the self-confidence necessary to become competent citizens of the modern world. Once different communities of modern people begin to assert themselves in transitional societies, the islands of stability which they represent may steadily expand; in time they can be joined together and, reinforcing each other, they will become the infrastructure of more modern and stable nation-states.[20]

So a band of professional teachers and educators (the colleagues in our "international teaching college") could become the nucleus of efforts to help create "communities of modernizers" who in turn would reproduce themselves, eventually without outside help. Professional teachers, above all, can disseminate the knowledge and skills necessary for living in the modern world; give to their students the psychological reassurance and support they need; hold their students up to exacting standards of achievement; display in their daily school life an image of what the professional at work is like; make of their schools or training colleges "islands of stability"; and thus help to promote the organization of the educational profession as a continuing and expanding community of modernizers. On this way to modernization lies freedom.

The right kind of teachers can be excellent modernizers, but to produce them we must also have excellent teachers of teachers. Both are literally worth more than gold—or loans—or commodities—or machines—in shaping the regenerative education that is so necessary for peoples who would be free as well as modern. The development of the right kind of teachers and of teachers of teachers is primarily the joint task of universities, institutes of education, and teacher training institutions. A key role should be played by the professional schools and departments of education.

I have tried to indicate in this book some of the ways that America should strengthen its troika in international education. Not least of the reasons for doing this is that such strengthening and coordination would aid other nations to produce an increasing flow of high quality teachers of their own. The American educational profession should mobilize itself for leadership in the international race for more and better teachers as a means to more and better education.

After all, the allusion to education as a race is not exactly alien to educational terminology. The very term "curriculum" itself had its origin in the Latin word currere (to run) and thus meant a running

20 Pye, op. cit., pp. 289–290.

or a race course. A "curricle" was a two-wheeled chaise drawn by two horses abreast. A curriculum therefore was the course or track upon which the curricles raced. By extension the curriculum became the course the school boy ran as he raced his way to an education. I would not try to carry the literary allusion too far. It might be argued that these days every horse-drawn vehicle is outdated no matter whether it be a carromata with a single pony, or a curricle with two horses abreast, or a troika with three horses abreast, or a quadriga with four horses abreast. I would not argue the point, but I would argue that America must strengthen its team in international education if we are to compete in the world's race for education with the wisdom, the speed, and the skill required of a modern and free nation.

The course for the educational race now extends around the entire world; a curriculum limited to Rome or Greece, to Europe or to America, to the West or to the East, to the North or to the South simply will not do for the future. While some may have doubts about whether the world stands to gain or to lose from an arms race or a space race, there is no doubt that the educational race is one from which the world stands only to gain.

Bibliography

Titles marked by asterisk contain extensive bibliographies.

ALMOND, GABRIEL A., and COLEMAN, JAMES S. (eds.), *The Politics of the Developing Areas.* Princeton, N.J.: Princeton University Press, 1960.

BARKER, H. KENNETH (ed.), *AACTE Handbook of International Education Programs.* Washington, D.C.: American Association of Colleges for Teacher Education, 1963.

BEALS, RALPH L., and HUMPHREY, NORMAN D., *No Frontier to Learning: The Mexican Student in the United States.* Minneapolis: University of Minnesota Press, 1957.

BENNETT, JOHN W., PASSIN, HERBERT, and McKNIGHT, ROBERT K., *In Search of Identity; The Japanese Overseas Scholar in America and Japan.* Minneapolis: University of Minnesota Press, 1958.

BLUM, ROBERT (ed.). *Cultural Affairs and Foreign Relations.* Englewood Cliffs, N.J.: Prentice-Hall, Inc., 1963.

Brookings Institution, The, *Development of the Emerging Countries: an Agenda for Research.* Washington, D.C.: The Brookings Institution, 1962.

Carnegie Foundation for the Advancement of Teaching, *The College and University in International Affairs.* Annual Report, 1959–60. New York: Carnegie Foundation, 1960.

CARR-SAUNDERS, A. M., *Staffing African Universities.* London: Overseas Development Institute, 1963.

CLEVELAND, HARLAN, MANGONE, GERARD, and ADAMS, JOHN CLARKE, *The Overseas Americans.* New York: McGraw-Hill Book Company, Inc., 1960.

COELHO, GEORGE V., *Changing Images of America: A Study of Indian Students' Perceptions.* Glencoe, Ill.: The Free Press, 1958.

Committee on the Foreign Student in American Colleges and Universities, *The College, the University, and the Foreign Student.* New York: The Committee, 1963.

Committee on the University and World Affairs, *The University and World Affairs*. New York: Ford Foundation, 1961.

*CORMACK, MARGARET L., *An Evaluation of Research on Educational Exchange*. Prepared for the Bureau of Educational and Cultural Affairs, U.S. Department of State, 1963, unpublished.

DAVIES, JAMES M., HANSON, RUSSELL G., and BURNOR, DUANE R., *IIE Survey of the African Student: His Achievements and His Problems*. New York: Institute of International Education, 1961.

FOSTER, GEORGE M., *Traditional Cultures: and the Impact of Technological Change*. New York: Harper & Row, 1962.

HAGEN, EVERETT E., *On the Theory of Social Change: How Economic Growth Begins*. Homewood, Ill.: Dorsey Press, 1962.

HALL, E. T., *The Silent Language*. New York: Doubleday & Co., Inc., 1959.

*Institute of International Education, Committee on Educational Interchange Policy, *College and University Programs of Academic Exchange*. New York: Institute of International Education, 1960.

Institute of International Education, *Open Doors 1963; Report on International Exchange*. New York, Institute of International Education, 1963.

Institute of Research on Overseas Programs, *The International Programs of American Universities*. East Lansing: Michigan State University Press, 1958.

ISAACS, HAROLD R., *Emergent Americans: A Report on 'Crossroads Africa.'* New York: The John Day Company, 1961.

KINCAID, HARRY V., *A Preliminary Study of the Goals and Problems of the Foreign Student in the United States*. Menlo Park, Calif.: Stanford Research Institute, 1961.

LERNER, DANIEL, *The Passing of Traditional Society*. Glencoe, Ill.: The Free Press, 1958.

McCLELLAND, DAVID C., *The Achieving Society*. Princeton, N.J.: D. Van Nostrand, Co., Inc. 1961.

MILLIKAN, MAX F., and BLACKMER, DONALD L. M. (eds.), *The Emerging Nations: Their Growth and United States Policy*. Boston: Little, Brown and Company, 1961.

*National Association of Foreign Student Advisers, *Research in Programs for Foreign Students*. New York: N.A.F.S.A., 1961.

Organization for Economic Co-operation and Development, *Policy Conference on Economic Growth and Investment in Education*, 5 vols. New York: OECD, 1962.

PYE, LUCIAN W., *Politics, Personality, and Nation Building*. New Haven, Conn.: Yale University Press, 1962.

RIVKIN, ARNOLD, *Africa and the West: Elements of Free World Policy*. New York: Frederick A. Praeger, 1962.

ROSTOW, W. W., *The Stages of Economic Growth: A Non-Communist*

Manifesto. Cambridge, Mass.: Cambridge University Press, 1960.

ROSTOW, W. W., *The United States in the World Arena: An Essay in Recent History*. New York: Harper & Brothers, 1960.

SCANLON, DAVID G. (ed.), *International Education; a Documentary History*. New York: Teachers College, Columbia University, 1960.

SHILS, EDWARD, *The Intellectual Between Tradition and Modernity: The Indian Situation*. Comparative Studies in Society and History, Supplement I. The Hague, Netherlands: Mouton & Co., 1961.

United Nations, Department of Economic and Social Affairs, *The United Nations Development Decade: Proposals for Action*, United Nations Document E/3613. New York: United Nations, 1962.

U.S. Advisory Commission on International Educational and Cultural Affairs, *A Beacon of Hope—The Exchange-of-Persons Program*. Washington, D.C.: U.S. Government Printing Office, April, 1963.

U.S. Department of State, Bureau of Intelligence and Research, External Research Division, *Language and Area Study Programs in American Universities*. Washington, D.C.: U.S. Government Printing Office, 1962.

USEEM, JOHN, and USEEM, RUTH HILL, *The Western-Educated Man in India: A Study of His Social Role and Influence*. New York: Dryden Press, 1955.

WATSON, JEANNE, and LIPPIT, RONALD, *Learning Across Cultures: A Study of Germans Visiting America*. Ann Arbor: University of Michigan Press, 1955.

*WEIDNER, EDWARD W., *The World Role of Universities*. New York: The McGraw-Hill Book Co., 1962.

Index